Matters of Life and Death

Other books by John B. Cobb, Jr.
published by The Westminster Press

Process Theology as Political Theology

Christ in a Pluralistic Age

With D. R. Griffin

Process Theology:
An Introductory Exposition

Matters of Life and Death

John B. Cobb, Jr.

Westminster/John Knox Press
Louisville, Kentucky

Scripture quotations from the Revised Standard Version of the Bible are copyrighted 1946, 1952, © 1971, 1973 by the Division of Christian Education of the National Council of the Churches of Christ in the U.S.A. and are used by permission.

Book design by Ken Taylor

First edition

Published by Westminster/John Knox Press
Louisville, Kentucky

PRINTED IN THE UNITED STATES OF AMERICA
9 8 7 6 5 4 3 2 1

Library of Congress Cataloging-in-Publication Data

Cobb, John B.
  Matters of life and death / John B. Cobb, Jr. — 1st ed.
     p.   cm.
  ISBN 0-664-25169-2

  1. Christian ethics—Methodist authors. 2. Life and death, Power over—Religious aspects—Christianity. 3. Sexual ethics. 4. Sex—Religious aspects—Christianity. I. Title.
BJ1275.C62   1991
248.4′87—dc20   90-19894

→* Contents *—

Introduction

As I have grown older I have become more and more concerned that theologians should address the most difficult and controversial issues of their day. I have become impatient with theologians, including myself, for our collective failure to do this. We seem to think that our special province is religion and, specifically, beliefs about God and human beings abstracted from the more immediate issues facing individuals and society. Since most people, including pastors, are not very exercised about these matters, we are generally left in peace to write our books in discussion with one another. By focusing on questions of methodology we can insulate ourselves even further from the concerns of church people and the general public. We complain at times about the reduction of Christianity to a private and subjective sphere, and we even criticize the church for accepting this limited role, but we do little to break out of our own ghettoized existence.

Of course, there is a high price to be paid if we reject this narrow role. Our academic colleagues do not recognize our work outside that role as theological, since theology as an academic discipline does not address these public issues. We do not have academic competence in relation to the topics we address, so we are likely to make embarrassing errors or express naive ideas. And we involve theology in controversy within the church, thus threatening the relative safety it enjoys when it is ignored. Furthermore, it seems that little can be gained. The authority with which theologians once spoke has long since eroded both in society and in the church. Hence a theologian cannot expect to have any significant influence on the course of events or even on church pronouncements.

Since the price is high, and there is little likelihood of

much influence, wisdom seems to support the prevailing silence. It seems that we theologians should know our place and stay there. If public issues are to be discussed, we should leave that to our colleagues, the ethicists.

The net effect of our collective silence, however, is that responsible contemporary Christian thinking is rarely brought to bear on the pressing issues that Christians and others face. I do not mean by this to disparage the statements of church leaders. Roman Catholics, especially, have not allowed contemporary theology to become entirely irrelevant to pronouncements on public issues, and from time to time the non-Catholic conciliar movement and individual Protestant denominations make helpful statements. But these statements rarely arise out of a healthy debate among the church's professional theologians, and their theological content is usually conventional. Inevitably, the majority of people, including the majority of church people, look elsewhere for guidance or simply consult their immediate feelings. It is time to risk another approach.

I am introducing this material in this way to indicate what I am, and am not, doing in this book. I *am* bringing my own theological point of view to bear on a range of issues that are intensely controversial in society today. I am *not* doing so with expertise in any of them. By a certain stretch of the usual application of the term, all the issues treated in this book can be called bioethical. A goodly number of Christian ethicists have specialized in bioethics. I have neither their experience nor the accumulated information that comes from long immersion in these issues. But, in general, positions on these issues reflect specialized information less than basic point of view. The question of basic point of view is, at least for Christians, a theological one. The following chapters treat a series of controversial topics from a point of view that is formed by a lifetime of reflection on the Christian faith.

The book takes up controversies in four areas. Chapter 1 discusses life in general and the place of human life within it. We Westerners have inherited a way of thinking that holds that there is a radical gulf between human life and all other forms of life. This can express itself in the idea that humans have both the right to live and the right to kill other animals with no compunctions at all. This drastic difference between human beings and animals of other species has been challenged and extensively debated in recent decades. The awareness that acting on the dualism of humanity and nature has done enormous damage for which human beings must pay a high price is forcing this reconsideration.

As part of this reconsideration philosophers have begun to debate the rights of individual animals. In public life the denial of rights to members of other species has been challenged also by a relatively small group of activists who are bitterly opposed to experimentation on animals and in general to the cruelties routinely inflicted on them by human beings. The actions of these activists, while often regarded as extreme, have served to focus media attention on these issues.

The church, meanwhile, which is often in the forefront of justice issues, has been silent with regard to how human beings should treat other creatures. It has begun to speak, belatedly, about the destruction of the environment in general, and this has included expressions of concern about the extinction of species. But the treatment of individual animals has not yet become a topic of discussion, much less of clear pronouncements. It is this topic that most clearly challenges the anthropocentrism that has dominated our ethics. Are Christians so committed to the view that other animals exist only as means to human ends that they cannot even consider the possibility that the torture of other animals is wrong, quite apart from its effects on human beings? The first chapter includes consideration of the human right to destroy the environment and exterminate other species, but its special focus is on the right of humans to kill individual members of other species or to cause them extreme suffering.

The second chapter deals with suicide. The title is not the right to commit suicide but "The Right to Die," because the issue today is not suicide in general but the right to terminate one's own life when it has become permanently meaningless and painful. The issue is often identified as euthanasia, but that suggests a focus on decisions made by some people about the life or death of others. The real issue now is the right of individuals to make decisions about themselves.

There is a growing weight of sentiment against forcing people to go through long periods of senescence, especially as victims of Alzheimer's disease. But there are also many who believe that their religious faith requires them to oppose any hastening of death. The stakes are high for millions of people. Yet the public discussion of a basic change of policy is in its infancy, and theological reflection is still minimal. This is an issue on which the mainline Protestant churches should take the lead, rather than wait until public discussion forces them to make reluctant and belated statements.

The third chapter discusses "The Right to Live," focusing on the issue of abortion. Today that is the hottest topic of all. The two sides seem to be polarized around mutually antithetical ethical principles. The division that arises in the society seems to be reflected in our Protestant churches as well.

Earlier much of the discussion in Protestant circles has treated the topic in terms of the rights of the mother. The issue is then presented as that of "the right to choose." Recently the pendulum has swung in church circles toward a focus on the rights of the fetus. Which approach is better is an open question, but without trying to settle that question, the treatment in this chapter reflects that shift. The issue is, then, whether, and in what sense, the fetus shares the general human right to life. How are its rights affected by the rights of others who are involved?

The fourth and final chapter is on sexuality. This is one

topic on which the church has certainly not been silent in recent years. But there has not been much active participation in this discussion by leading Protestant theologians. In mainline Protestantism the recent flurry of study and talk comes after a long period of silence, during which one group of Christians assumed that the Victorian ethics of their youth were self-evidently what the church stood for and another group assumed that the church had accepted the sexual revolution.

Ironically, the contemporary debate in the church was precipitated more by the demand of homosexuals for ordination than by a general sense of responsibility to give guidance to Christians in this central area of their lives. The church was caught unprepared, and its debate has taken place in relation to an issue that should appropriately have been brought up in a context of some consensus on sexual morality in general. It is too late for that rational approach to be possible, but it is not too late to discuss the more general principles.

The church's theologians have not done much to guide the church through this muddle. Activity by theologians could not have prevented the present agony, but it might have helped. It might help even today. At least theologians have the obligation to try.

Although the chapter offers some general ideas relevant to thinking about sexuality, most of the attention is given to two topics that are particularly controversial today. The first is premarital sexual intercourse. The second is homosexuality.

This chapter is entitled "The Right to Love." Whereas the first three chapters are quite literally and directly speaking of matters of life and death, one could argue that this one is not. Sexual activity is not strictly a requirement of biological life itself for the individual involved. Nevertheless, many readers may agree that, in a less literal sense, sexual expression is also often felt as virtually a "matter of life and death."

Few if any of the ideas offered in these chapters are radically new. Still there may be value in sorting out the issues and coming to a consistent way of thinking about them. Beyond that, the claim is that this consistent way of thinking can justify itself as one legitimate expression of Christian faith.

By no means do I consider these views the only possible Christian ones. That kind of exclusivism is too arrogant to be Christian. For those who have been sensitized through ecumenical discussion, and through the experiment in theological pluralism that has characterized the past century, the claim to have the one true answer appears idolatrous. It introduces a taint of fanaticism into the discussion and action that helps no one. My purpose is to propose one Christian perspective, the one, namely, that has commended itself to me over the years.

Positions on the issues discussed in these chapters are often presented in relation to deeply moving accounts of the suffering of animals, women, cancer patients, fetuses, homosexuals, and so forth. These stories are useful in gaining attention to the topics and showing their importance. We think most vigorously when we feel keenly. On the other hand, at this stage part of the problem is that emotions are often too strongly involved in the positions taken, and the need may be to view these issues in a somewhat more detached way. Accordingly, I have done little to involve the reader's emotions. It is my hope that readers will be aware of the high stakes that are involved in these decisions, and that my failure to spice the argument with moving stories will not be taken for lack of feeling on my part. Some questions can be decided more fairly at some remove from the urgency of individual cases.

My reflection over these years has been deeply influenced by Alfred North Whitehead. I mention him in this book only here, but perceptive readers will note his influence. For the most part his influence is negative. Whitehead has taught me to reject dualism, anthropocentrism, substantialism, and essentialism. Since the discussion of the subjects dealt with in this book is often affected by dualism, anthropocentrism, substantialism, and essentialism, the rejection of these "isms" does lead to a distinctive perspective and treatment. The Bible has often been read through some combination of these "isms," and in my view its message has been distorted thereby. But my appeal is to the intrinsic sense of what is said, not to the authority of a philosopher.

Whitehead's influence also appears in my understanding of the relation of God and the world. He has taught me to understand that God is in the world and the world is in God. God's grace is God's own presence in the world, and God is genuinely empathetic with the world, rejoicing with those who rejoice and suffering with those who suffer. I find this message in Jesus, and it deeply informs my understanding of Christian faith and its ethical expression. Some of my argumentation in the chapters that follow depends on this understanding of God and the world.

The danger of emphasizing that there is a plurality of views responsibly held by Christians is that it seems to open the door to complete relativism. That is in no way the true meaning of pluralism. Relativism in this debilitating sense is not possible for the Christian. But that does not throw Christians back on absolutism. There are good theological reasons for rejecting that also. Only God knows the final truth. For human beings to pretend to stand in the position of God is not acceptable. Humans are finite, fallible, sinful vessels of God's grace. Their grasp of truth is fragmentary and distorted. To recognize that fact, deeply, enables one to think in less fragmentary and less distorted ways, but it does not enable one to escape from one's creaturely condition.

Once all have set aside every pretense to know the final truth, the real discussion among Christians can begin. Even then, by no means every position put forward by one who belongs to a Christian church can justify its claim to be responsibly Christian. Theological pluralism can never mean that every opinion is as good as every other! My claim that I am presenting a responsible Christian view of these difficult issues is a bold one.

Further, I do not present my viewpoint as simply one among others from which I invite the reader to choose arbitrarily. I present my views as the best I can attain, after considering at least some of the others, and I invite others to join me in them. But these views are grounded in the understanding that they are highly fallible, that I have much to learn from others, and that other Christians as committed and responsible as myself disagree for reasons that are as convincing to them as my reasons are to me. In the text I have deleted all the phrases that emphasized that what I write is an expression of my perspective: "in my view," "it seems to me," "as I see it," and so forth. To introduce those phrases here and there may give the impression that elsewhere I suppose myself to have transcended this relativity. But the reader should understand that even the most dogmatic statements can be nothing more than the expression of my considered opinion.

For the present these considered opinions are quite convincing to me. And as long as I am convinced that this perspective is the most appropriate one for me as a Christian to adopt, not only will I hold it myself, but I will act on it and try to persuade others to do so as well. But I hope I will never view those who disagree as less human, as less worthy of respect, or as less Christian than myself simply because they are convinced by different arguments.

The whole discussion in this book is in the language of rights. This is certainly not the only possible approach to these topics. The chapters could have been entitled instead: "Overcoming Dualism and Anthropocentrism," "Death with Dignity," "The Love of Infants," and "Sexual Fulfillment." Those titles would have led to discussion of quite similar topics, but they would have shaped the treatment differently.

I have chosen instead to stay with the language of rights, for two reasons. First, it is the language in which most of the current discussion in our society occurs. To shift to other categories makes one's position in the current debate less clear. Second, although the language of rights distorts the discussion by focusing it on individuals, it also highlights very real and important issues that are sometimes obscured by other approaches. Those other approaches include some more natural to me. I am adopting the language of rights so as to direct my own attention to just these issues.

The language of rights has been used to limit the exercise of coercive power. If the nobles have certain rights, as the Magna Charta declared, then the king, despite superior force, is not permitted to act so as to violate those rights. Of course, he may do so anyway. But once the idea of those rights is well established, their violation is likely to arouse a degree of opposition from all who possess them that must give the king pause. Further, the king himself may internalize the idea of these rights.

The rights of the nobility may be initially granted by the king or won from him through confrontation. During the Enlightenment, thinkers sought to ground rights more objectively. They argued that human beings, or at least some of them, are endowed with rights by God or, when God-language seemed problematic, by nature. Certain rights resided intrinsically in individuals—usually in adult males, often restricted to Europeans, and sometimes only to those possessing sufficient property. All those meeting the necessary qualifications had such rights as "life, liberty, and the pursuit of happiness." Governments, therefore, had the responsibility to uphold those rights and were forbidden to infringe upon them.

In the nineteenth and twentieth centuries these rights have been extended so that today ethnicity and gender are no longer viewed as determinants of rights. Also, new rights have been added. In many societies it is now assumed that everyone has the right to sufficient food and access to medical care simply by virtue of being human. Freedom to worship as one chooses, or not at all, is also widely considered a basic right. All adults are thought to have the right to participate in selecting their rulers.

Nevertheless, the actual meaning of affirmations about rights is obscure. Is it really meaningful to assert that nature or God endows people with rights, or that an individual, simply by virtue of being human, possesses rights? Clearly such an assertion cannot mean that all human beings have been recognized as having rights, have themselves claimed such rights, or have been able to exercise them. To assert a right is not really a descriptive statement. It is, instead, a normative one, expressing the judgment that human beings should be viewed and treated in a certain way. But it is a normative statement that refuses to be interpreted positivistically. That is, it denies that the norms are matters of personal taste and preference. It affirms that there are inherent characteristics in human beings that ground and demand these normative judgments.

But just what can this mean, or how can it be justified? The clearest interpretation is that the affirmation of a right is a shorthand way of describing duties owed to an individual by all other people, duties that are derivative from the nature of that individual. These duties are, for the most part, negative. If I have the right to life and liberty, then you have the duty not to kill or enslave me. Further, your duty is not a function of what is required for you to improve your character or to attain to happiness. It is a function of my worth or potentiality. It is for my sake and not yours that you have a duty not to kill or enslave me. It is, therefore, equally the duty of everyone, regardless of diverse perspectives and interests. The fact that you do not share the perception of me as a person worthy of life and liberty does not justify your infringing on these rights of mine. In this sense my rights are objective.

It would often be convenient and advantageous for those possessed of coercive power to ignore and violate the rights of one person or another. Often this happens. But the affirmation of the rights of these people forbids such conduct, and the moral power of society as a whole defends these rights even at considerable cost.

The book is not a study of the moral and legal meaning of rights. In this respect it leaves most questions unanswered. These few paragraphs are intended only to indicate the perspective from which the language of rights is used. From this perspective, taken alone, the assertion that a deer has the right to live means that neither I nor any human being should kill it, and that the reason for this is to be found in the deer's own being and value. Taken alone, the assertion that human beings have the right to kill deer means that morally and legally there should be no restrictions on human killing of deer for the sake of the deer. There may still be restrictions assuring that the killing of deer will be sufficiently limited so that deer will survive for the sake of future hunters.

Just as competing rights may be attributed to human beings, so in this case there remains the possibility that both affirmations may be legitimately made. If so, then the respective rights must be adjudicated. The result is likely to be that people may kill deer under certain circumstances, but that additional restrictions are imposed on the killing, this time not for the sake of other hunters but for the sake of the deer. For example, those who adopt this position may justify hunting deer for food but oppose hunting them for sport.

In previous centuries, when attention focused on a very few rights, and these very fundamental, it was natural to treat them as almost absolute. To this day, the claim to a right tends to carry with it the claim that this right should supersede all other rights. This absolutist tendency built into the language of rights arouses strong emotions and makes reasoned discourse about competing rights difficult. For example, those who speak of the right of the woman to decide about what happens in her womb seem to be in total opposition to those who speak of the right of the fetus to life. One way to prevent this tendency toward absolutism is to avoid the language of rights altogether. One could simply ask in each instance what is the best course of action for all concerned. But to change the language in this way would be to sidestep many of the current debates. A second way, the way adopted in this book, is to accept the formulation in terms of rights and then to work against the individualism and absolutism so easily associated with it.

The following chapters are slightly revised versions of the Caldwell Lectures given at Louisville Presbyterian Seminary in March 1990. Their origin as lectures may be apparent to the reader. The hospitality of the Louisville faculty and community was outstanding, and the critical response to the lectures was helpful. I would like to take this occasion to say a heartfelt thanks to all involved.

Earlier versions of some of the lectures were given at other places: Brite Divinity School, Iliff School of Theology, and at a conference held at the School of Theology at Claremont. I am grateful to those schools also for the encouragement and helpful criticism I received.

John B. Cobb, Jr.

ONE

The Right to Kill

———⚜———

The Biblical Evidence

What are Christians to say about the relation of human life to other forms of animal life? Is the dualism inherited from centuries of Christian theology as well as from modern philosophy the final word? Do human beings have an unlimited right to exploit natural resources, to destroy the habitats of other species, to inflict suffering on individual animals and to kill them? How are Christians to go about answering these questions?

There is no one theological method that can be applied equally and directly to every issue that arises. For example, the direct appeal to the Bible is not always useful. There are issues that were so remote from the minds of the biblical authors that looking to their opinions for guidance is artificial. There are other issues on which scientific and historical information available to us, but not to the biblical writers, or new applications of the principles of justice and liberation, make it impossible to take their opinions as authoritative. There are still other issues on which biblical authors take quite diverse positions, and there is no one method on which we can all agree in order to adjudicate the issues.

Hence, the traditional appeal to the authority of the Bible cannot be the one method for the solution of all current problems. Nevertheless, it is a good rule for Christians to consider the biblical contribution to the discussion first, when there is such a contribution. There are some topics on which the Bible speaks with considerable clarity and consistency and on which modern science and historiography shed little new light. At least on those issues the biblical view has great authority for Christians. The relation of human beings to other living things is one of these. Hence this chapter begins with the biblical witness.

The topic is not discussed in the Bible in a direct and thematic way. Yet views of animals are expressed here and there, and on the main issues confronting Christians today what is expressed seems generally consistent. The most important and influential passage comes at the very beginning. It has often provided a springboard into this discussion, and it can do so here as well. The story of Creation is familiar, but it repays careful rereading.

This story can be used, and has been used, to emphasize the gulf that separates human beings from the remainder of the created world. Only human beings are created in the image of God, and only human beings are given dominion over all things. These two distinctive features of humanity are closely connected. Dominion is a divine prerogative. For God to share it with human beings, or perhaps even to delegate it to them, is an amazing honor. In part, at least, to be created in the image of God is to have the status of ruler. Even if it is not defined in this way, it involves this status in a most intimate way.

Given this contrast of human beings as participating in lordship over all else, on the one side, and all other creatures as subject to that rule, on the other, a dualism of ruler and ruled can be derived from the Genesis passage. This has been developed into the view that human beings have the absolute right to do with the remainder of the created order, including all other living things, as they please. Being in the image of God, it is argued, human life is of unlimited intrinsic value. Given over to human rule, all other life is merely instrumental to human ends.

With little resistance from theologians, modern philosophy carried this dualism still farther. Descartes radically distinguished mental from physical substances, and he attributed the former only to human minds. Other living things are simply complex machines. Kant's position is systematically even more extreme. He viewed the human mind as the creative source of its world. What is given to the mind is a noumenal reality that has no discriminable character whatsoever. The status of other animals is not an important topic for Kantians, but the implication is that their existence, apart from the human experience of them, is wholly beyond human ken. In subsequent idealism, even the noumenal reality of the external world disappears.

Until recently, philosophical ethics was quite consistent with these metaphysical assumptions. Ethics had to do only with human relations with other people. Relations with physical things, including animals, had importance only insofar as these things were property or otherwise valuable to people. An occasional recognition that animals might also be considered morally appeared in footnotes, but this had no effect on the course of discussion.

Theologians have sometimes objected to human beings arrogating to themselves functions that belong to God alone. But there has been little protest against emphasizing the uniqueness and utter superiority of human beings within the created order. The idea that human life is sacred has been a modern axiom, usually affirmed by theologians as enthusiastically as by secular humanists. Indeed, Christians have often tried to gain credit in secular eyes by claiming the Bible as the source of this idea. They trace it to the doctrine of the *imago Dei*, that is, the idea that humans, and humans alone, are created in the image of God.

Thus one source of the inherited dualism between human beings and other animals was the influence of the Bible, and Christians rarely protested as the dualism received still more radical formulation in modern philosophical thought. Christianity has thereby played an important role in justifying a treatment of animals that has shocked many sensitive consciences. Although in the 1920s some churches acknowledged the moral importance of the treatment of animals (cf. "Humane Education: Animals Have Rights,"

Church and Society, vol. LXX, no. 1, pp. 26–27), dominant Christian teaching still depicts these disturbed consciences as reflecting unwarranted sentiment rather than justifiable moral outrage. The question now is whether this is the final word for Christians to speak on this topic.

Surely it is not! Although this biblical story certainly does single out human beings as those with whom God is peculiarly concerned, the Christian habit of accenting only this one point reflects more an arrogance that is not commended in the Bible than a balanced reading of the story. To take an analogous instance from the teaching of Jesus, that a human life is "of more value than many sparrows" (Matt. 10:31) does not warrant the conclusion that sparrows are worth nothing at all. Indeed, it presupposes the opposite. The heavenly Father cares even for sparrows; how much more for human beings! This certainly means that people too should be more concerned about a human being than about a sparrow. Much more! But it does not warrant the teaching that sparrows exist only as means to human ends.

The dualism of ruler and ruled, from which the other dualisms have developed, is not denied by the assertion that even the sparrow has some worth for God. But reflection on dominion, as that is understood in the Bible, does not support the metaphysical and ethical dualisms to which it has given rise. It certainly does not support the exploitation of the ruled by the ruler! God is not indifferent to those over whom God exercises dominion. On the contrary, God is pictured as loving the creatures and caring for them, not only human beings, but the sparrows as well. If the dominion humans receive from God is a sharing in God's dominion over all things, then it is not rightly expressed in treating those over whom human beings have dominion as mere means to human ends. It should be expressed in concern for the well-being of the subjects. Casual cruelty is not justified, and the systematic ignoring of this casual cruelty that is characteristic of the church's thinking to date is not derivable from the *imago Dei* and the dominion connected with it.

To consider this further, turn again to the first chapter of Genesis, where both the *imago Dei* and human dominion are introduced. Is its central point the difference between human beings and everything else? This is certainly *a* point. But this point is located in a context that has been largely lost in the course of Christian thought. This context focuses on the goodness of the whole creation. Exegetes have sometimes read this passage as if it said that the whole of creation is good as a locus for human life, that its goodness is relative to human beings. But the text does not say this. On the contrary, God *sees* that the created order is good quite apart from the presence of human beings within it. This means, in philosophical language, that all creatures have intrinsic value.

Within the whole of the nonhuman creation, animals are singled out for special consideration along with human beings. To both, God gives plants as food. Nothing is said at this point about the eating of animals either by human beings or by other animals. It is also striking that the commandment to be fruitful and multiply is given first to the creatures of the sea and the air. There is no suggestion that giving the same command to human beings abrogates the earlier command to these other creatures, or that granting dominion to human beings authorizes them to prevent other living things from fulfilling this commandment.

It is not possible here to survey the whole biblical literature on this question. But it may be worthwhile to look at one other story, the one that deals most explicitly with animals—the story of Noah and his ark. This story, too, certainly indicates that God has concern for other species as well as human beings. Indeed, the emphasis is on the preservation of species.

Today there is much interest in the preservation of species. Often the argument is that such preservation is for the sake of the human future, but sometimes biodiversity is affirmed as of value in itself. The Noah story supports both points. God commands that seven pairs of clean animals be saved and only one of unclean (Gen. 7:2). The importance of the clean animals for human use justifies their larger numbers. Nevertheless, the preservation of the unclean points to the intrinsic value of maintaining the diversity of species independent of human use. When the ark has landed, God commands Noah: "Bring forth with you every living thing that is with you of all flesh—birds and animals and every creeping thing that creeps on the earth—that they may breed abundantly on the earth, and be fruitful and multiply upon the earth" (Gen. 8:17).

A further point of interest in this story is that the covenant that God establishes with Noah, promising that no such disaster will ever again be inflicted on the earth, is also "with every living creature that is with you, the birds, the cattle, and every beast of the earth with you, as many as came out of the ark" (Gen. 9:10. See also Gen. 9:12 and verses 15–17). It is particularly interesting that this affirmation of all living creatures as covenant partners with God comes immediately after the reemphasis on human dominion and the *imago Dei*.

What does this biblical vision imply with respect to the human right to kill other creatures? The issues here are varied and complex. Some focus on the question of killing in terms of degrading the biosphere generally. Others focus on the extinction of species; others, on the killing of individual animals. What rights do humans have in all these respects? What are their limits? On these issues it may prove illuminating to locate Christian thinking in relation to two well-articulated positions that have been staked out by others: on the one side, a challenging form of what is called "deep ecology," and, on the other side, a strong defense of animal rights.

Deep Ecology

The first section explained how the Bible opposes the anthropocentric view of other creatures, that is, the view that they have value only for human beings. God *sees* that they are good without any reference to human beings. When the Creation is completed, God views the whole and *sees* that it is very good. Not only are individual species and their members of value in themselves individually, but the total creation with all its complex patterns of interdependence has a value that cannot be reduced to that of its individual members. In the story of Noah, God shows care to preserve all the species threatened by the flood, calls for them all to be fruitful and multiply, and establishes a covenant with all.

Although deep ecologists do not base their views on the Bible, they could gain support from some of these features of the Genesis account. Their approach is to argue that it is indeed the complex interrelated whole that is of supreme value. Further, the way in which individuals and species contribute to this whole is by playing their assigned roles, occupying their assigned niches, interacting in their assigned ways. Human beings constitute one of these species. For hundreds of thousands of years, as hunters and gatherers, human beings functioned as one species among others. They thus contributed to the richness of the whole. This was the world that, in biblical terms, was "very good."

But at some point, perhaps ten thousand years ago, human beings began to overstep the boundaries, to cease to function as merely one species among others. They began to domesticate other species. In the process they also "civilized" or domesticated themselves. They became alienated both from the inclusive creation and from their own natural being. They undertook to gain mastery over themselves and over the remainder of creation. They prided themselves on their ability to objectify and control themselves, including their interior lives.

In short, from this deep ecological perspective, human beings made themselves sick and mad. They often sought healing by intensifying just those things that had made them sick. The so-called "higher" religions intensified the self-transcending that separated human beings from the remainder of creation and from their own real nature. They began to seek a home in another world or in an imagined future on this planet. Their alienation from themselves led to mutual hostility, exploitation, and violence. They dismissed as "primitive" those peoples who continued to live in a natural and healthy way and, having dismissed them, they committed, and are continuing to commit, genocide against them.

The only real hope, then, is to reverse the whole process of history and civilization, to recover the latent naturalness within. This leads to a renewal of a self-understanding of human beings as simply one species among others. People would cease to claim any special status, special privilege, or special responsibility. Human beings would defend themselves, as all creatures do, and use other species as needed, as all species do. But they would not claim any special right to do so. And they would respect the other species as they defend themselves against human beings.

What steps could be taken to make this kind of world possible? The first would be to preserve and to extend wilderness. The number of domesticated animals would be reduced in order to make space for wild ones. Meat would be increasingly obtained by hunting instead of by husbandry. And human beings would progressively overcome the habits of mind and social practices by which they have domesticated themselves inwardly and outwardly.

This deep ecology position is that of Paul Shepard, one of the most profound thinkers about the relation of human beings to other species and the natural world in general. (See especially his *Nature and Madness*; San Francisco: Sierra Club Books, 1982.) Not all who identify themselves as deep ecologists agree with Shepard in detail, but no one provides a more radical challenge to Christian believers. The issue now is, What can a Christian say in response to him? When Christians give up their long-established anthropocentrism, is this where they go?

Christianity and Deep Ecology

Shepard's position can readily be laid alongside the biblical myth. It is an account of an initial paradise and an actual fall. In many respects it parallels the biblical account. It differs in that in the biblical Garden of Eden, human beings did not hunt the animals. It was simply a gathering society; Shepard more realistically posits a hunting and gathering society. But otherwise, the parallels are close. In the biblical account the domestication of plants and animals is associated with the fallen condition and is immediately connected with violence among human beings. Further, the tree on which the forbidden fruit was found was the tree of knowledge of good and evil. The eating of that fruit fits well with the self-objectifying or self-transcending that is, for Shepard, the heart of what is wrong with civilized humanity, what estranges human beings from their naturalness.

Does this mean that the Bible, rightly understood, supports this kind of deep ecology? In some ways it does, but there are two main differences. First, even before the Fall, human beings, although certainly one species among others, were also differentiated from the others. They were not *merely* one species among others. Human beings, and they alone, were created in the image of God. They were assigned a particular privilege and a particular responsibility. Christianity has historically been cursed by a misreading of the specialness and an abuse of human privilege and responsibility. That abuse began in the Fall. It has become more serious throughout history down to the present day. Overcoming that abuse is now the task of all concerned human beings, and for Christians that means a profound repentance. But the idea that human specialness is itself the problem, that people should stop thinking of themselves as especially privileged and responsible in relation to other species, cannot be derived from the Bible.

The second point of difference is closely related. Christians may agree that the Fall is closely connected with a kind of self-understanding that disrupts a purely natural attitude. This is surely implied in the eating of the fruit of the tree of the knowledge of good and evil. But in the biblical tradition the goal is not to return to the state of innocence that preceded this knowledge. The angel guards the entrance to the garden, so there can be no turning back. Ironic though it may seem, the way forward is not a reduction of understanding of good and evil, a lessening of self-transcending, but a deepening of knowledge.

The difference here could be put in theological terms as follows. For Shepard's deep ecological position, the Fall is an unmitigated disaster. The only possible form of health is the one that was lost in that Fall. Our only hope is to return as far as that is possible to the earlier condition. For Christianity, the Fall is ambiguous. Something of great value was lost. Life since the Fall has been beset by terrible evils. But the salvation that is mediated to humanity by Christ exceeds in value the innocence that preceded the Fall.

This means that there are two sharply opposed views of history. It would be hard to disagree with Hegel that history has been "the slaughter-bench at which the happiness of peoples, the wisdom of States, and the virtue of individuals have been sacrificed" (G. W. F. Hegel, *Reason in History*, trans. Robert S. Hartman; New York: The Liberal Arts Press, 1953, p. 27). Hegel was thinking only of the mutual destruction of human beings. Those sensitive to the wider creation must add the slaughter of other species and the destruction of the health of the biosphere. The horrors that human beings have inflicted and are now inflicting on the whole of creation can hardly be exaggerated. Christians bear heavy responsibility for the continuation of these horrors. Nevertheless, Christians do discern in the course of events something other than progressive evil. In Christ, Christians find a whole-making process whose potential, at least, is to attain something greater than what was originally lost. What Christians find in Christ is a deepening wisdom that involves a heightened self-transcendence rather than a return to innocence.

The practical implications of Shepard's deep ecology and the Christian view are, therefore, different. Christians seek a future wholeness that includes in a new synthesis elements of what has come into being since the Fall as well as elements of what existed before. The inclusion of elements that have come into being throughout history is viewed, not as mere concession to necessity, but as a joyful and grateful expression of appreciation for what has been achieved by God in and through fallen human beings. For example, the knowledge of nature gained by science should inform us ever more deeply. But the appreciation and understanding of the environment of primal peoples should be recovered and renewed in creative synthesis with what the natural sciences have learned. What we have discovered about the curative power of certain chemicals is certainly worth remembering, but this modern medicine needs to be integrated with primal wisdom about the body and its health and ways of being in the natural world. More generally, the wisdom of primal people needs to be recovered within the context of a self-consciousness and self-knowledge hard won through human history.

These differences also affect attitudes toward the question of animal rights. From the point of view of many deep ecologists, sensitivity to the suffering or killing of individual animals is an anthropomorphic mistake. It is the extension to them of human-centered ideas. This ethical and legal way of thinking expresses the loss of naturalness that is deplored. It is suspect even in its application to human beings. But to extend to interspecies relations what has its limited value within the human context only worsens the situation.

To respect the other species is not to treat them anthropomorphically. The need is to appreciate them in their otherness, not to exaggerate their similarities to the human species. Human beings should not take on responsibility for other creatures. Instead, by accepting the human condition as one species among others, humans can leave to other species their own destiny. In any case, the problem is that we have degraded other species by domesticating them and are now extending this degradation to the remaining wild species by trying to "manage" them. Thus, in the view of deep ecologists, the problem is not that individual animals are denied their rights. The problem is that human beings have rejected their allotted place in the scheme of things and have undertaken to control the whole.

The Christian has good reason to share with Paul Shepard and other deep ecologists the concern about the degradation of other species involved in their domestication. The species seen as good by God were wild. The extension of wilderness so as to share the world with wild species more equitably, and thus allow them to fulfill God's command that they be fruitful and multiply, is eminently desirable. Dominion has been badly, even perversely, expressed in the degradation and destruction of those over whom it is exercised.

Nevertheless, after Christians have acknowledged the profound truth in the insights of deep ecologists, they must disagree. Human beings *do* have dominion. The question is not whether they should maintain it or should relinquish it, as the deep ecologists favor. The question is how human beings should exercise this dominion. They *are* responsible. And to carry out their responsibility, they do have to ask what rights other creatures have vis-à-vis them. How *ought* human beings to treat members of other species? Should they treat these other creatures in the way deep ecologists favor, as others, in relation to whom interspecies rivalry is appropriate? Or, given the enormous advantages human beings have in that rivalry, should they recognize that other creatures have rights over against them that should limit human use of superior equipment? What uses of these creatures are justified? What uses are not justified?

Deep ecologists are correct that wilderness should be extended and renewed. But even this extending and renewal is an expression of human dominion, now rightly exercised. The same dominion requires ethical decisions with respect to the preservation of species and the treatment of individual animals. In short, the issue of animal rights is important for Christians. To refuse to assume responsibility, on the ground that taking responsibility is the problem, would be to leave the field to the irresponsible. Human beings have dominion, whether they want it or not.

Animal Rights

The animal rights movement is quite different from deep ecology. It shares with Christianity the assumption that human beings do have dominion and that the issue is how to exercise it. The movement has arisen out of concern for the suffering that human beings inflict on individual animals, chiefly domesticated ones. This concern is viewed as sentimental by many deep ecologists, who see the suffering of individuals as simply a necessary part of the system that generates vitality and complexity in the whole. Christians can agree with deep ecologists that some in the animal rights movement have so focused on individual animals as to ignore the more serious question of the destruction of habitat for wild animals, with the resultant decimation, and even extinction, of whole species.

But Christians also have reason to take seriously the questions raised by committed defenders of animals, and to be grateful for their passionate concern. Society as a whole has been acting out its anthropocentric perceptions in ways that have been brutal indeed. They have been applied to the production of meat for our tables and to the use of animals for educational, experimental, and entertainment purposes. Unlimited torturing and killing have been practiced without even asking whether it served any important human purpose. The church has stood silently by and even actively supported the cruelty. Christians have little basis for criticizing those who, with greater sensitivity, have forced them to attend to these matters.

When Christians finally enter this discussion, what position should they adopt? Does the acknowledgment of the intrinsic value of every creature entail the consequence that human beings do not have the right to kill any of them?

The argument against the human right to kill typically begins with the widely held assumption that everyone knows that killing another human being is always wrong. Each human being has the right to live. This has been undergirded by the idea of the *imago Dei*. It has also been reinforced by the Christian doctrine of human dignity derived from the idea that each human being is a child of God. Christians and many others have taught that the right to live is an exclusively human possession. The question is whether this radical line between human beings and other species is justified.

Believers in animal rights sometimes describe this position as "speciesism." They argue that just as it has been hard to overcome the view that only whites have the right to freedom because of their superior race, or males have the right to dominate because of their superior sex, so it is hard to overcome the view that only humans have the right to live because of the superiority of their species. But reason works against such a drastic distinction between "us" and "them."

When whites were forced to acknowledge that blacks shared all the relevant human characteristics, they had to back down on their justification of slavery. When males are forced to acknowledge that females have all the relevant human characteristics for participation in public life, they have to back down on their justification for denying women equal political and legal rights. When humans are compelled to acknowledge that other animals share the characteristics relevant to the right to life, humans will have to back down on their arrogant assumption that they, and only they, have the right to live and hence that they have the right to kill other animals.

The form of the argument is valid. The question is whether in fact other animals, or some of them at least, do share the relevant characteristics, that is, those characteristics of human beings that ground the human right to live. To arrive at a rational conclusion on that issue requires the specification of these characteristics.

Some may be disposed to argue that the only relevant characteristic is simply humanness or belonging to the human species. Those who adopt that line are "speciesists." That is, they are frankly asserting that commonality of species is the basis of rights, as whites have sometimes asserted that being white is the basis of rights, and males that being male is the basis of rights. But most theologians and philosophers have gone beyond this to identify characteristics of human beings that entail the right to live.

Theologians often appeal to the *imago Dei*. There is nothing wrong with that. But unless one operates in a purely authoritarian fashion, one must go on to say what feature of humanity is pointed to by this term. If it is reason, then one must acknowledge that some nonhuman animals participate more in the *imago Dei* than do some members of the human species. The same is true if one identifies the *imago Dei* with the ability to speak and to understand language.

The argument of those who oppose the human right to kill animals of other species is that people do not think of the right to life as restricted to those members of the species *Homo sapiens* who are clearly rational or who are able to use language. Infants and persons with severe brain damage also have the right to life. Hence, it seems that the basis of the right to live is something more elemental. Some propose that it is the capacity to have interests. If so, this is clearly shared by many animals. To hold that human beings, because they have interests, should not be killed, whereas other animals with analogous interests may be killed with impunity, is speciesism. And, of course, speciesism is an irrational prejudice that should be overcome.

Christianity and Animal Rights

How should Christians respond to this line of argument? They have no reason to reject the general form of the argument. But they do have reason to reject the absoluteness that it presupposes and employs. Taking the right to life of every member of the species *Homo sapiens* as an absolute sets up the debate in an unhealthy way.

This absolutistic thinking is widespread. Among Christians it is often thought to be required by the Bible. Certainly biblical commandments against murder are typically stated without qualifications. For example, and most influentially, in the Ten Commandments the prohibition is stated quite simply, "You shall not kill" (Ex. 20:13). Few dispute that in context this means that people are not to kill other people.

Absolutistic interpretation of this and other commandments, or of the modern reformulation in terms of rights, has played an important role in history. Sometimes it has functioned to protect the powerless against the powerful. It functioned to muster the forces of opposition to slavery and to extend rights to women. In some measure it limited the exploitation of indigenous peoples by colonialists. It has protected infants, including deformed infants, from destruction. It expresses itself in the prohibition of abortion and even of contraception. It supports laws against the taking of one's own life, regardless of one's suffering. It sometimes leads to keeping alive human bodies in which there is no longer any distinctively human faculty.

To whatever extent Christians base this absolutism on the Bible, their arguments are weak. The Israelites who accepted the Ten Commandments as central for their covenant with God did not understand them to preclude killing as a form of punishment or in war. Subsequent chapters will consider how they applied this prohibition, if at all, in certain borderline instances. In any case, deriving rules of present behavior from ancient laws, treated as absolute, is a form of legalism specifically criticized by both Jesus and Paul. Of course, the general point that people should not go around killing one another is overwhelmingly valid. If Christians derive their behavior from love of God and neighbor instead of from specific rules, this does not encourage murder!

To assert that Christians should not argue from the absolutization of traditional laws does not mean that they have not done so. Christians have developed legalisms again and again that have the absolutistic character criticized by Jesus and Paul. Nevertheless, the argument for such absolutistic use of ancient laws is weak. Shifting the discussion from law to rights does not, from a Christian point of view, justify the absolutism that often accompanies Enlightenment discussion either.

Once such laws are taken as absolute, the use of intelligence in their application in various contexts becomes difficult. The only way of discriminating among the implications drawn from them, supporting some and opposing others, is by asserting that in one instance or another those who are protected are not human. For example, those who advocate allowing human bodies to die when they no longer support consciousness are often forced to deny that these bodies are human. But in some sense they certainly are. If the absoluteness of the human right to life, as of all rights, is set aside, then a more reasonable discussion of the merits of each case is possible.

If human beings do not have an absolute right to life, members of other species do not either. This does not necessarily mean, on the other hand, that other animals have no right to life at all. Indiscriminate killing of these other creatures for minor human purposes may not be justified! A more careful analysis of the circumstances under which killing is wrong in general can indicate whether these circumstances arise only in the human case or also with other creatures.

There are three reasons why it is extremely important to forbid the killing of human beings in ordinary circumstances. First, killing brings an end to a series of personal experiences that, if continued, have unique and irreplaceable value. Second, the fear of being killed profoundly reduces the enjoyment of life and the ability to make one's own decisions freely and creatively. Third, the death of one person disrupts the lives of others and contributes to their suffering. These reasons are so important that it is the first duty of every society to assure the basic security of its members against random killing.

But it is also obvious that if reasons such as these are the ones that lead to the prohibition of killing or the affirmation of the right to live, then they do not apply equally in extreme cases. A human vegetable can be killed without ending a series of irreplaceable experiences, since those have already ended. A person who wants to die does not fear death so much as continued living. There are those whose death disrupts the lives of others very little and may even be a relief to those most closely involved.

If the right to life is based on considerations such as these, does it apply to nonhuman animals? In some cases the answer seems to be negative. It is very doubtful that the death of an oyster ends a uniquely valuable series of experiences. If it makes way for another oyster, nothing of great value is lost. It is extremely doubtful that an oyster's life is much affected by anxious anticipation of death. And there is no indication that the oyster's death leads to grieving on the part of other oysters. At the other end of the spectrum, the answer seems quite clearly positive. Among chimpanzees and whales individual differences are significant, and the death of one seems to be experienced as a real loss by others. To what extent the anticipation of death affects the quality of life is harder to say, but to suppose that there are analogies to the human experience is safer than simply to deny it. If the considerations listed above are the basis for the right to life, then members of these species do share that right with human beings.

This is not the place to try to apply these considerations to every species. But the general implication is that the right to life applies much more to gorillas and dolphins than to chickens and sharks. Permitting tuna-fishing, while trying to reduce the killing of porpoises that accompanies it, makes sense from this point of view.

Those who argue in this way are often accused of having failed to escape an anthropocentric point of view. They are told that they are making judgments based on human values. It is correctly pointed out that from the point of view of the chicken, the shark, or the tuna, it is their lives that are most important, not those of human beings, chimpanzees, whales, and porpoises.

It is true that the judgment that some animals have more right to life than others is based on very fallible human perceptions. In that sense all human thinking is necessarily "anthropocentric." But that is not what is reasonably meant by anthropocentricity. The issue is not whether all human thinking is human. Of course it is. The issue is whether human thinking can acknowledge that other creatures have value apart from their value to human beings. It can. Human beings have sufficient capacity for self-transcendence to recognize that other animals have such value and that human thinking about them should begin with that recognition.

The question remains whether human thinking in this way gives any greater validity to human judgments than chicken "thinking" in its way gives to theirs. This argument is not silly. Every reason given for favoring human modes of thought over those of chickens turns out to be circular. If there are only multiple perspectives, then it can be argued that every perspective is as true as every other. The claim that one's own perspective is privileged can be seen as arrogant. This argument can be finally overcome only if there actually is a privileged perspective.

From the Christian point of view there is a privileged perspective, that of God. In some Christian formulations it seems to be privileged only because God has the power to carry out God's purposes so that others are forced to conform. But such worship of coercive power is not truly Christian at all. Instead, God's perspective is privileged because God is omniscient, in the sense that God's perspective includes all others. It includes both the perspective of human beings and that of chickens. The divine experience includes both that of the shark and that of the whale. The judgment that the death of the whale precludes further experiences of much more distinctive value than does the death of the shark is, finally, a judgment about their respective contributions to the inclusive whole which is the divine life.

Elements of a Christian Ethic

This chapter has focused on the right to kill. The argument has been that human beings do have the right to kill members of many other animal species. But those creatures which, like ourselves, have individual distinctiveness in experience, those that can be affected by fear of death, and those whose deaths lead to the suffering of others have the right to life in much the same sense as do human beings. Those who have seen *Gorillas in the Mist* or studied marine mammals in any detail are likely to understand and appreciate such an affirmation of rights.

Although this chapter does affirm, with many qualifications, the human right to kill, it does *not* affirm the *duty* to kill. Even if human beings have the right to eat pork, or chicken, or beef, they certainly do not have the duty to do so. One is free to be a vegetarian, thus reducing one's participation in one large system of killing. Indeed, there are a number of excellent reasons to make this choice over and above the desirable reduction of killing that it supports. As the production of adequate food for a growing world population becomes more difficult, there will be more and more reason for eating grains directly instead of feeding them to livestock. Even today much livestock-raising is ecologically destructive. And there are definite indications that large consumption of red meat is unhealthful.

With most animals, the right that human beings have the greatest duty to respect is not the right to life but the right to be relatively free from suffering. This is underscored by the Christian understanding that God suffers with all creatures in their suffering. To inflict suffering on a calf is to inflict suffering on God as well.

Of course, suffering is part of life in the wild, and it is not the duty of human beings to alleviate that. But it is the duty of human beings not to inflict additional suffering on fellow creatures for trivial purposes. These creatures have the right not to be tortured by human beings. The violation of this right is massive, and Christians share in responsibility for the extent of its violation in both past and present.

From the beginnings of domestication of animals, interest in their freedom from suffering has been subordinated to economic considerations. One should not minimize the suffering that has been inflicted on these creatures throughout the centuries. But with the advent of factory farming, the evil has been terribly accentuated. Animals are treated as machines for meat production. The personal relation with animals characteristic of traditional small-scale farming is gone. Quantitatively the suffering of these creatures is vastly increased. It is difficult to justify participating in a system of food production and consumption, as meat eaters do, that involves such suffering.

In defense of present practices it is sometimes pointed out that if human beings did not find domesticated animals useful, there would be far fewer of them. This point was made by Samuel Johnson. "There is much talk of the misery which we cause to brute creation; but they are recompensed by existence. If they were not useful to man, and therefore protected by him, they would not be nearly so numerous." To this Boswell replied, "But the question is whether the animals who endured such sufferings of various kinds, for the service and entertainment of man would accept existence upon the terms on which they have it." (Quoted by John Bowker in *Animal Sacrifices: Religious Perspectives on the Use of Animals in Science*, edited by Tom Regan; Philadelphia: Temple University Press, 1986, pp. 12–13.)

The issue between Johnson and Boswell is a serious one.

Certainly if there ceased to be any demand for beef or leather, cattle would be slaughtered or simply left unattended. Their numbers would be greatly reduced. Perhaps their existence does compensate them for a certain measure of suffering and for untimely death. But against this argument it should be noted that a great decrease in their numbers would allow an increase in the number of the wild animals they typically displace and that it is reasonable to think that the enjoyment of life on the part of these wild animals is considerably greater.

Even if Johnson's argument can be taken to justify a certain amount of suffering, Boswell's reply surely is decisive in application to the calves now raised for veal in totally unnatural circumstances. Their existence is misery. For them death is a friend, perhaps the only friend. They emphatically have the right not be treated in this way.

What then of the human right to enjoy tender veal? Surely human beings do have the right to enjoy good food. The issue is whether this right outweighs the right of the calf to a life free from unreasonable suffering. The issue here is not, then, the right to kill calves. Assuming that the potential experience of individual calves is not remarkably distinctive, that fear of death is not an important factor in their lives, and that the death of the calf does not cause major distress to others, a calf could be killed after a reasonably enjoyable life and human beings could still have veal. The issue is whether the difference in tenderness and price involved in this different way of raising calves justifies the imposition of so much suffering. It does not.

If this judgment is not to be purely private and idiosyncratic, it needs, in principle, to appeal beyond the perspectives of the calf and the veal eater. For the Christian, this appeal is again to the divine perspective. God experiences with the veal eaters their gustatory delights. God also experiences with the calves their lifelong misery. The former fall far short of balancing the latter.

Theism and the Rights of Species

Belief in God also illuminates another important issue, that of the extinction of species. Many people are concerned about the decline of biodiversity resulting from human destruction of the habitats of myriad species. But is there any real justification for this concern? Is it sheer sentimentality?

When the species that die out are animals that people enjoy seeing, it is easy to argue that their disappearance is a loss to future humanity. But if they are species of which only a handful of specialists at most have any knowledge, species that would be unattractive to most people if known, then this kind of reason has little weight. In a nontheistic context the argument must be that these species have potential scientific or medical value to future generations. But in many instances this is not convincing either.

If the destruction of species entailed the reduction of life on the planet in a quantitative sense, then another kind of argument could be made. One could argue that intrinsic value is being reduced. But this is not necessarily the case. With the extinction of one species, others may multiply. There may be no reduction in the total quantity of intrinsic value in the world. Indeed, if the extinction of other species makes possible a larger human population, then it could be replied that the total amount of intrinsic value is increased.

If it could be claimed that these species play an irreplaceable role in the ecology such that their disappearance threatens the health of the biosphere, a strong argument could be made against their elimination. The drastic reduction of biodiversity now taking place does give reason to fear for the health of the biosphere. But only in rare cases does the elimination of any single species threaten the whole. The real intuition is that diversity in itself has value, that it enriches the whole.

The argument for maintaining diversity is strong to whatever extent the diversity is known and enjoyed by human beings. Human experience is certainly impoverished when the forms of life with which human beings come into contact, directly and indirectly, are reduced. But much of the diversity, in fact most of it, is not even known to human beings. In any case, the number of species is so vast that the human mind is not really able to appreciate it except in the most abstract sense. If there is no appeal beyond the human enjoyment and use of biodiversity, then the loss of many species is of trivial importance.

The intuition that the diversity is of value is really the intuition that it contributes to the value of the whole, that the contrasts of the elements making up the whole have value for the whole. That implies, in principle, that the whole is not merely the sum of the parts but also a unity that includes those parts in their diversity and in all the patterns of relationship that are enriched by diversity. This requires that there be an inclusive perspective in addition to the innumerable fragmentary ones. In short, it makes sense to one who believes in God.

Concluding Comments

Human beings do have the right to kill many other animals. But, like all rights, this one is limited in many ways. Human beings have the right to use creatures of other species for human ends, but they should not use them as if they existed for human purposes alone. They have value in and of themselves apart from their value to humanity. The human use of these animals always involves some element of loss, and the suffering they experience is an intrinsic evil. Further, that suffering is shared by God. When Christians forget that, as most of them have forgotten through most of Christian history, legitimate use becomes illegitimate exploitation.

It is a sad commentary on the limitations of Christian self-transcendence that Christians did not notice their abuse of the environment until they were forced to recognize that the consequences of that abuse threaten human well-being in a massive way. Now they need to establish new guidelines for their interaction with the rest of creation. These will involve principles about maintaining a healthy biosphere, slowing the extinction of species, and reducing the suffering of those animals on which their actions most directly impinge.

None of these new principles can be implemented without profound changes in habits of mind and style of life. The human quest for the good life will continue to degrade the environment unless the understanding of the good life changes. Humans will continue to exterminate other species at a rapid rate unless they respect wilderness and reorder their economies and their societies accordingly. Hundreds of millions of creatures will continue to suffer unnecessarily unless people understand that that suffering is evil in itself and causes suffering to God as well.

Such generalizations do not decide most of the specific issues. Many of these are complex, difficult, and legitimately controversial. The argument of this chapter is that these issues *are* morally important and that the time is now past when they can be ignored by Christians. Once Christians admit their responsibility to think these matters through, they will have much to contribute.

Christians can affirm the human right to kill. But surely that by itself is a poor expression of Christian faith, hope, and love. The right to kill must be set in a much wider context of responsibility to contribute to the welfare of other creatures as well as of human beings. When this is done, the possibility of a healthier biosphere, with greatly reduced suffering on the part of its nonhuman members, will arise. May it be soon!

TWO

The Right to Die

---※---

Situating the Christian Discussion

Although the right to die has been a concern of some people for a long time, the intensity of interest has grown for several reasons. First, issues related to the termination of the lives of those who want to die are being discussed in the public media and, in specific cases, decided in courts of law more often than in earlier decades. Second, as medicine keeps more and more people alive, the number of persons who live longer than they wish under the conditions to which they are condemned increases. And third, more and more people, seeing the victims of such diseases as Alzheimer's, feel strongly that they do not desire to live on in such a condition.

There is a prima facie case favoring one's right to die rather than being forced to live on in a degenerating condition, should these become one's only options. First, the dread of living on in that way casts a shadow over one's life, a darker shadow, in many cases, than any cast by the expectation of death itself. This shadow could be removed only by a clear public decision that one could choose not to continue to live in that condition. Second, long-protracted life as an Alzheimer's patient is a heavy burden on one's family, with virtually no compensating rewards. Third, the social resources devoted to caring for one patient could be put to far more beneficial uses.

The apparent implication is that once it became clear that degeneration of this kind was the only destiny one could anticipate, one should be free to decide whether to submit oneself to that fate or to terminate one's life before the disease was so far advanced that one could not participate in the decision. One should be able to seek guidance from those best qualified to know as to the appropriate time and as to how best to die with dignity and minimal pain. It should be socially acceptable for others to assist one in this termination. One could, therefore, assemble one's family and closest friends and bid them farewell before taking the poison or being injected with an appropriate drug.

Because this seems to me a far better scenario than what now routinely occurs, the question is why it is still so rarely even considered. Why does society assume that it has the responsibility to keep one alive even against one's desires and to the benefit of no one? Why does society insist that one has a duty to live on under these conditions? Why do individual persons not have the right to decide?

Chapter 1 began with an appeal to biblical authority. It argued that biblical teaching on the relation of human beings to other animals is fairly consistent and that the situation with respect to these relations has not changed in ways that invalidate the biblical view. But the case is different on the topic of suicide and, indeed, on the topics of our third and fourth chapters as well.

There is no consistent biblical teaching on taking one's own life in extreme circumstances or even on assisting another to do so. Saul is neither commended nor condemned for killing himself to avoid capture, and if his armor bearer had acceded to the request to assist him in his suicide, it is not clear that he would have been commended or condemned either. Other biblical stories can be cited for and against the legitimacy of suicide in the eyes of biblical authors.

Furthermore, the topic of this chapter is not the sort of suicide of which there is any consideration in the Bible. The situation that raises the issue of the right to die for us is a new one. The great problem in biblical times was that so many died before their time. For biblical writers, when death came after three score and ten years there was a natural sadness over the loss, but the death was not thought of as evil. Today there are many means of keeping people alive that were unknown in earlier generations. Many of those who live into their eighties and nineties and beyond celebrate much of this extension of life. But environmental stresses combine with this longer life to cause many to suffer for years with degenerative diseases. As a result a whole new range of issues has arisen. The Bible is an important source for dealing with these issues, but it does not speak directly to them.

The following consideration refers to the Bible from time to time, but it is organized in terms of the kinds of objections to the right to die that often arise in discussions within the church. Three confused objections are treated briefly, first, before five serious arguments against the right to die are considered. The chapter concludes with some comments about the context within which the discussion must now proceed if it is to be adequate and honest.

The first of the three confused objections to the right to die appeals to the shock of the family members. Someone might point out that some members of the family would be horrified at witnessing the suicide or hearing about it, and that one has no right to inflict that shock upon them. Given the present climate of opinion, that reaction is certainly possible. But that is no reason to oppose the effort to change the climate of opinion and the legal structure that expresses and enforces it. In fact, apart from that climate, the shock of observing the death is likely to be much less than the shock of watching the degeneration over a period of years.

The second confused objection is that we can never be certain of a diagnosis. Perhaps one's destiny would not be in fact as bad as expected. One's suicide would then have prevented one from making some further contribution to society or from enjoying life oneself. The answer is that, of course, mistakes are made. One would need to know that possibility when making one's final decision, so that one could take it into account. If the chance that the diagnosis may be wrong leads one to decide to continue living, fine. The point here is only that one should make that decision for oneself.

Finally, people are likely to object that this is euthanasia, and that euthanasia involves decisions by one group of people about the life and death of others. The issue of euthanasia cannot be avoided, but it is not the one here in view. The issue here is one's right to die, one's right, that is, to make a decision to end one's own life, not someone else's right to decide whether one lives or dies. The question is not whether others have the right to kill one who wants to live, but whether they have the right to force one to live when one wants to die.

Playing God

The first of the serious arguments that are truly directed against the right to die is that human beings should not "play God." In antiquity most people were convinced that the course of history, and even of individual life, was basically in the hands of superhuman powers. Human beings knew that their efforts had little effect on the larger course of events. This was determined by chance, or by fate, or by the gods. The Christian affirmation was that, despite all appearances, the determination is made by a personal God who cares for each creature and ensures a just outcome for all and a happy one for believers. This came as very good news.

In this context, notions of divine election, predestination, and providence were joyfully accepted, and they resonated with much of human experience. Accordingly, it seemed wrong to "play God" in the sense of trying to replace God as the primary determiner of the course of events. Of course, that never meant that people did not try to benefit themselves or protract their lives when they could. It meant only that, individually and collectively, they judged that their ability to determine their own destiny was secondary to the determination by superhuman power.

But we live in a very different world. For two centuries people have "played God," in the sense of taking human destiny into human hands. Since the French Revolution, Westerners have believed that human thought and action can shape and reshape the social, economic, and political order in fundamental ways. The experiment has had mixed results. The future has become more precarious. Today it has become apparent that human decisions and human hands can cause the ultimate holocaust, and many feel regret at the loss of an earlier innocence.

On the other hand, few would willingly give up the enormous advances in medicine. Most people favor "playing God" to prolong lives by inoculations against diseases, by taking medicine when they are sick, and by keeping people alive who would die without human intervention. People also "play God" in family planning, thus avoiding unwanted children. Most believe in "playing God," even to the extent of killing those who want to live—in war, in self-defense, and in punishment of crime. The taboo against "playing God" now focuses almost exclusively on ending a life for other reasons. Specifically, opponents of the right to die argue that allowing persons to end their own lives, or, even more, helping them to do so, would be "playing God" in an objectionable sense. Yet why apply this ancient taboo only in this one instance—to a problem largely created by "playing God" in so many other ways? To leave life and death to natural processes has a certain consistency. To exercise human control has a certain consistency. But to exercise human control at all points except one, and to forbid it there, requires justification that cannot be found in a general prohibition against "playing God."

Before leaving this argument, however, it will be well to consider the specific form given it by that most influential of theologians, Thomas Aquinas. He wrote:

What makes a man master of himself is having free will. He may accordingly manage his life in respect of all those things which may go to make up his life, and this is the province of his free will. The passage from this life to a more blessed one is, however, not a matter subject to man's free will, but to God's power. A man may not, therefore, kill himself in order to escape from any of the miseries of this life. (*Summa Theologiae*, Part II–II, Q. 64, Art. 5. Blackfriars in conjunction with Eyre & Spottiswoode, London, and McGraw-Hill Book Company, New York, 1975.)

In support of this position, Thomas states: "God alone has the authority to decide about life and death, as he declares in Deuteronomy, *I kill and I make alive*" (Deut. 32:39). Except for quoting that biblical text, Thomas offers no argument. It is simply understood that whereas within the parameters of life free will has an important role, life as such is a gift of God that can be legitimately ended only by God.

Although this sense that the beginning and end of life are wholly in God's hands may once have been plausible, it is today certainly not self-evident. The citing of a biblical text does not clinch an argument of this sort, especially since in the Bible itself suicide is not clearly condemned. Theologically, few now would accept the view that one range of actions belongs wholly to the sphere of human free will and another wholly to God. God is at work everywhere, but in a way that does not set aside the decisions of the creatures. Instead, God makes such decisions possible and works in and through them.

Human Life as Sacred

A second argument against the right to die is that human life is sacred. This sacredness of human life, or infinite value of the human soul, has been a core belief of much of the modern world. The terms "sacred" and "infinite" are designed to do away with all conditionals. Human life is not to be respected only when it is happy, healthy, or virtuous, or when it belongs to those of one's own religion or race. Its claim is unqualified. This means that no one has the right to destroy a human life, even one's own.

This absoluteness, if taken with complete consistency, leads to conclusions drawn only by a few. These oppose not only capital punishment but even killing in self-defense or in defense of loved ones. They refuse to participate in military activities even in defense of their homelands. The great majority of Christians, in contrast, qualify the absoluteness of the affirmation for practical purposes. When the killing of some is necessary to save the lives of others, they believe that society must weigh the consequences of killing and of not killing. Even capital punishment of the guilty is sometimes defended, if it may deter the murder of the innocent. National defense is generally allowed and supported even at the cost of killing millions of people.

Despite these qualifications, adherents of the view that human life is sacred, or of infinite value, continue to draw the conclusion that society has the duty to keep its members alive regardless of their own desire to live or die. The duty to sustain life is seen as more fundamental than the duty to respect the preferences of the people involved. It is life that is sacred, not personal freedom to do with it what one wants.

This feature of modern thought must be taken very seriously. It stands in the way of implementation of another major tendency in the modern world—the technocratic and bureaucratic reduction of human beings to mere means to political ends, or to resources for the economic system. Black slavery and native American genocide have provided unforgettable glimpses, in the history of the United States, of what happens when some human beings are excluded from absolute respect. In this century German Nazis provide a still more vivid picture. Clearly the absoluteness of the value of human life has never been consistently acted on. But, equally clearly, it has been an important conviction leading to desirable laws that protect the unpopular and check the exploitation of the weak by the powerful. If the acceptance of the sacredness of human life is the only way of preserving these benefits, then the price of being denied the right to die must be paid. But it is yet to be shown that only absolutist formulations can protect against these evils.

The preceding paragraphs have asked: What are the gains and losses involved in the sacralizing of human life? Because of the importance of these pragmatic considerations, another cost, the topic of chapter 1, should be noted again. Historically the sacralizing of *human* life has been accompanied by the reduction of all other forms of life to mere means to human ends. All inhibitions about inflicting suffering on our fellow creatures have been ridiculed as sentimentality. It is hard to know how to weigh, against the gains for human beings, the costs to other creatures of viewing human life as sacred. But the costs should be recognized and emphasized. Further, the cost of brutal treatment of other animals is not only to them. Brutality to others brutalizes its perpetrators.

Some of those who are disturbed by the gross inhumanity of human treatment of other creatures have proposed the extension to all living things of the sacralizing now applied only to human beings. Schweitzer gave classic expression to this position in his doctrine of reverence for life.

This proposal is worthy of full consideration in its own right, a consideration that involves many of the issues discussed in chapter 1. In any case, the implications of sacredness are inevitably modified in the process of attributing it to all living things. In a world in which so much of life depends on the destruction of other life for its sustenance, declaring that all life is sacred cannot result in extending to all living things the protections that have been accorded to human beings based on the idea that only human life is sacred. Indeed, when the continuity of all life, implicit in Schweitzer's formulation, is thought through, the absoluteness of the human right to life has to be qualified also. If it is

life as such that is sacred, and if the sacredness of life cannot, in view of the needs of others, mean that each living
thing should be kept alive, then sacredness does not imply
the right to life except in a quite relative sense. This relativ-
izing effect of extending sacredness to all life is sometimes
given as a pragmatic reason for limiting sacredness to *human* life, but this kind of argumentation cannot escape the
charge of speciesism explained in chapter 1.

However, the doctrine of the sacredness of human life is
not defended only on pragmatic grounds. Those who dedicate themselves to it believe it is not only useful but, in
some profound sense, also true. They *see* each person as
deserving of utter respect or reverence. This is an axiom or
fundamental intuition, not just a useful slogan.

This conviction comes from religious sources. The Stoics
were among the first Westerners to articulate the idea that
there is a divine element in every human being and to draw
implications from that. The New Testament emphasizes
that God's love for every human being is independent of
any deserving on that person's part. It draws the conclusion
that those whom God loves should be loved by Christians
also. The first chapter of Genesis provides a ground for all
of this in the doctrine of the *imago Dei*. Whatever continuity there may be between human beings and other creatures,
there is also, in the biblical view, a special relation of human
beings to God. Although modernism tried to establish the
sacredness of human life without reference to God, Christians have generally supported the doctrine on the basis of a
deeper grounding than atheists can provide.

Does this mean that in fact Christians have no choice but
to support the sacredness of human life and the implications
drawn from it, including the denial to individual persons of
the right to die? No, this does not follow. First, on purely
theological grounds, the doctrine of the *imago Dei* is not
equivalent to the sacralizing of human life. Strictly speaking,
in biblical terms, only God is sacred. Human beings, whatever their special relation to God, are not sacred. The *imago*

Dei is not a spark of the divine in the Stoic sense. The primary focus of the first chapter of Genesis is not the separation of human beings from the remainder of creation but the goodness of the whole. Again and again, God sees that the creation is good quite apart from the presence of human beings. What is finally seen to be *very* good is the whole creation inclusive of human beings, not human beings alone. It is true that dominion accompanies the *imago Dei*, as what is distinctive of human beings, but the biblical principle is that dominion, especially when modeled on divine dominion, is for the sake of the ruled. It cannot justify exploitation of the ruled by the ruler. It does not introduce the kind of dualism between human beings and all other creatures that has characterized so much of Western thinking, especially since Descartes.

The point of this brief reminder of matters treated more fully in chapter 1 is not to deny that modern humanism, with its sacralizing of human life, derives much of its force from a secularization of biblical teaching. It does. But through that secularization the teaching is changed. What belongs only to God is attributed to human beings. The depth of distinction that applies only to the relation of Creator and creatures is applied to the gap between human beings and other living things. Although Christians are committed to a teaching that affirms respect for every human being simply as human, they are not committed to the sacralizing of human life or to the affirmation of the *infinite* value of each human life. Christians need to recover a more biblical way of affirming respect for every human being simply as human. Such an affirmation need not have the negative consequences of the exaggerated, even idolatrous, formulations that have characterized modern thinking.

A better formulation can begin, as the Bible does, by affirming the goodness of all creation. In the first chapter of Genesis, we can also discern certain gradations of value and importance. Although the inanimate world is good in itself, and certainly this holds true for plants, something more is added when animal life appears. Plants are good in themselves, but they are also good as food for animals, including human beings. Human beings are part of the whole system of creation, but they also have a special role to play in the whole, one that relates them to God in a distinctive way. Accordingly, people should have respect for the whole created order, and they should exercise their dominion responsibly and carefully to ensure the continued goodness of that order. They should be particularly concerned with the life-system and, within that system, that animals of all species be able to be fruitful and to multiply. Certainly they have their greatest responsibility toward members of their own species. The question is how to formulate that responsibility in a way that does not work against human responsibility to other creatures and that does not inflict suffering unnecessarily on people.

At this point Christians can turn to the New Testament for guidance. There an idea drawn from the Jewish Scriptures is emphasized in many ways, the idea that God loves all people, and that people should love one another. What action follows from love for another human being? Love can usually be expressed best by allowing that other human being to realize her or his own projects so far as these do not prevent other persons from realizing their projects also.

The qualification "usually" is needed, because there are times a person is acting against her or his true interests. Although experience has taught that very often the interference of one person in another's affairs is damaging, there are exceptions. If someone's project is to stay high on drugs, it may be proper to try to redirect that person to getting treatment instead. In short, love allows the one loved to realize her or his projects except when the lover judges that the cost to that person and to others is unacceptably great. The lover may judge that the deeper project of the one loved is being thwarted by the immediate and more controlling project, and the lover may intervene for the sake of the realization of the deeper project, for example, the project to attain a more enduring happiness than drugs can offer. On the other side, sometimes simply "allowing" is too little, and love expresses itself in active helping or, in extreme cases, even implementing another's project for her or him. But in the overwhelming majority of cases, allowing is the best that can be done, and what should be allowed is that the other act freely based on the other's judgment of interests.

Application of this principle to the issue of the right to die does not establish that right as absolute. One may judge that, even if someone has decided that she or he wants to die, the cost of that death, either to the person in question or to others, is unacceptably great. It is not difficult to think of situations in which that judgment would have widespread support. For example, if a middle-aged man with a family to support finds life extremely difficult and unpleasant and decides that the easiest way out of his problems is death, most reasonable people will do what they can to persuade him against that option and even to block it if they can. The cost to the family would be too great both in financial and in emotional terms. Even if his life is painful, he would have the obligation to struggle with his problems rather than to escape them at the cost of imposing still greater hardships on others. Friends may also judge that in the long run the man himself can yet gain much satisfaction from continued living.

Nevertheless, when the principle is stated in this way, rather than in terms of the sacredness of human life, the burden of proof falls on the one who would prevent others from following their own desires. Further, the argument could not take the form of specifying that it is always wrong to shorten one's life voluntarily. Genuinely to respect another person, as love requires, is to accept that person's right to make judgments about what she or he is to do. It is interference with the other's decisions that requires special justification.

On the one hand, no one has an absolute right to act on her or his preferences, because one may be making a mistake in judgment even about one's own interests, and especially because the effects on others should be considered. On the other hand, there is no basis for appealing to absolute prohibitions against taking one's own life. In the particular case proposed, if the man is succumbing to Alzheimer's disease, the chances are that his responsibilities to others and to himself jointly support the decision to end life with dignity and without pain before the disease has run its course.

Emotional Consequences

The third argument against the right to die that must be taken quite seriously is that deeper than the practical advantages of having a loved one live or die are emotional attachments. Even when the quality of relationship that evoked the love may no longer be possible, the love retains its force and is directed to the living body. Even after death, some of these feelings attach to the corpse and then to the place where the body is buried. Many people are drawn to visit the graves of their loved ones. In extreme cases, these feelings about the body lead to its preservation and to pilgrimage to its site so that it can be seen. Since the feelings involved are so deep, to ask a person to participate in the decision to terminate the life of a loved one, or even to acquiesce in that decision, is a cruel demand. Natural and desirable human feelings call for the affirmation of life, not death. One needs to believe that the death of the loved one has come in spite of all efforts to maintain life, not, even in part, as a result of one's own decision.

These natural and healthy feelings are strengthened by a view of the world that modernism has made dominant. It is the view that the most real things are enduring physical bodies. These are in motion relative to one another, and, indeed, this matter in motion *is* the reality. All else is the by-product of this motion. The physical body, then, *is* the person to whom attachment is felt. That body is not just what or who it is now in its present condition, but precisely that person whom one loves, inclusive of the history of loving relations. To destroy that person now is to destroy the underlying reality of all that one cherishes from the past.

This worldview is quite the opposite of the Platonism that still exists alongside materialism. For Platonism, the reality of the person is to be found in the soul. The soul's relation to the body is secondary, so that a certain contempt for the body is not inappropriate. Personal attachment is then properly directed to the soul. In extreme cases, when the body seems to have only vegetative existence, the Platonic understanding can lead to total indifference to it, and to the belief that it can be killed with impunity. But usually the results are remarkably similar to those that follow from the materialism, for it is supposed that in the Alzheimer's patient, to continue with this example, the soul remains, and *is* the person who is loved.

Both of these views are substantialist. That is, they identify the "really" real with something that endures unchanged beneath the changing surface of things. The natural attachment to the person is directed by this way of thinking to this underlying substance, whether physical or mental. This counts against the decision to end its existence, even when the present form of that existence is negative both for the person in question and for others.

Another way of thinking is more realistic. The deepest reality here involved is the flow of experience of the loved one and of those who love. Much of that experience, especially in its intimate interconnectedness, is very precious. But it is past. As past, it is still real and effective in the present. But that reality and effectiveness are not dependent on the continued presence of the living body. There are also present experiences, and there will be future ones. It is these about which decisions need now to be made, not about a substance underlying all experience. Real love for the other is derived from the past, but it will lead to focusing on what is happening now and on what will happen in the future. The past will not be changed.

This does not invalidate the natural and healthy feelings that the body does evoke. They are profoundly intertwined with the way the past enters into the present. But realizing that the past continues in the present, quite apart from the continuing presence of the living body of the loved one, can help to encourage a natural and healthy letting go.

The Slippery Slope

The fourth main argument against the right to die is that once the door is opened to individual cases of suicide or euthanasia, there will be no clear place to hold the line. It is supposed that the results of such a lack would be so disastrous that it is better to hold to an absolute or retain an ethos in which such issues are not allowed to arise. The proposal in this chapter is that suicide be accepted as a basic right to be opposed only when it can be shown that the legitimate needs of others, or the deeper interests of the person contemplating it, outweigh the right. If this proposal were adopted, it is objected, the question of whether to kill oneself might be considered almost routinely whenever one is in acute trouble. Society cannot count on people in that situation either to reflect clearly themselves or to turn for help and advice to others who would bring real wisdom to bear. Furthermore, if one person's death seemed advantageous to another, there would be nothing to prevent the one who had something to gain from it from putting the idea of suicide in the other's mind and suggesting that there might be a moral duty to carry it out. Especially with the aged, the line between their suicide and their murder by others would often be hard to establish.

Or consider matters from a slightly different point of view. What message does society want to give its members with regard to the value of human life? At present the consensus of Western culture is that society should communicate its almost unqualified affirmation of each individual human life. That "almost" is a necessary qualification has been emphasized above, and there is no need to repeat that discussion. What is communicated by law and rhetoric is that each individual human life is to be protected except under truly extraordinary circumstances. This means also that each individual is to treasure her or his own life as well as that of others.

This message from society to its members is an appropriate and valuable one. Hence, it is argued, any change in laws and mores with respect to ending one's own life could only serve to weaken a desirable ethos. Children growing up in a society in which they heard talk of the right to die would think of life and the importance of maintaining it differently. They would not prize life quite so much, either in themselves or in others. As they face painful crises in their own lives, the question of why they should go on with life would become a more natural and inevitable one. The simple answers now available would be gone. The already alarming rate of adolescent suicides would increase.

Even if the argument for the right to die is made originally only in favor of those who have had a full life and face an irreversible and degrading decline, there would be some carryover to different circumstances. Even worse, there would also be some carryover when the question had to do with terminating the lives of others involuntarily.

This kind of argument must be taken seriously. Absolutes have their function in society. Ideally mature people do not need them, but ideally mature people are rare. Most people are helped in avoiding pitfalls by rules that they lay down for themselves or that society lays down for them, rules that work well in the great majority of instances. If the instances in which people are justified in wanting to die are rare, then maintaining the absolute prohibition may be warranted. In this way society can avoid the complex problem of regulating the consequences of a fundamentally different ethos. If all these advantages can be gained, the cost of having a few people forced to live longer than they want is a small one to pay.

But the number of cases in which people are justified in wanting to die is far from insignificant. Hence, it is time to begin constructing a system of thought and law that struggles with the ambiguities and uncertainties that acknowledgment of the right to die unquestionably involves. The task now is to find a rhetoric and a moral code that affirm the right to die without undercutting the emphasis on the preciousness of each individual person. As advances in medical science cause more and more people to live on after life has lost its meaning, this will become increasingly important. It is not unachievable.

Suicide as Unnatural

The fifth and last of the arguments against allowing people to choose death is that suicide is unnatural. Historically this may have been the most influential argument of all. Thomas Aquinas provided a strong formulation of this point as his first reason for opposing all suicide.

> Everything naturally loves itself, and it is for this reason that everything naturally seeks to keep itself in being and to resist hostile forces. So suicide runs counter to one's natural inclination, and also to that of charity by which one ought to cherish oneself. Suicide is, therefore, always a mortal sin in so far as it stultifies the law of nature and charity. (*Summa Theologiae*, Blackfriars edition, Part II-II, Q. 64, Art. 5.)

This argument, like the many similar ones that have appeared since the time of Thomas, is odd. It seems to be an argument that no one would ever choose to die more than that one should not be allowed to do so. But if, in fact, no one ever chose to die the argument would not be needed.

Of course, defenders of this argument know that people do choose "unnatural" things. Thomas and those who follow his line of thought argue from a natural tendency to a moral requirement in such a way that exceptions to the tendency are treated not merely as unusual but as morally unacceptable. This is the "natural law" approach.

Natural-law theory has had a long and honorable history. It has often functioned as the only check on purely positivistic views of law, namely, that laws are whatever those who rule a people decide that they should be. When positivism is accepted, if those who rule declare that all left-handed persons are to be killed, such killing becomes just. From the point of view of natural-law theory, such law can be declared unjust and evil and can therefore be vigorously opposed.

Unfortunately, natural-law theory has also functioned in repressive ways, especially in the area of sexuality. It has been declared that by nature the function of sexual intercourse is procreation, so that sexual intercourse has its only justification when this intention is present. This illustrates the arbitrary element in determining what the "laws" of nature are. Obviously sexual intercourse is sometimes ordered to procreation. Equally obviously, much of it is for the sake of mutual enjoyment. Who is to say that one is natural, the other not?

Thomas and the theistic writers who have followed him do provide a basis for the move from what is usual to what is morally mandatory. They believe that the intentions of God can be read through a study of creation, and that thereby the "natural" can be judged "normative." If one can discern from the observation of nature that procreation is *the* purpose of God for sexual intercourse, then one can argue from the divine purpose to the moral conclusion that it is wrong to engage in intercourse for other purposes. This argument is a tenuous one, but theism does provide a context in which a case for it can plausibly be made. When analogous arguments about what is "natural" are found in nontheistic writers, they are puzzling indeed. Yet even atheists who feel a revulsion against certain types of behavior often oppose them as "unnatural" and hence immoral.

Theologically, the argument against Thomas must be that Christians should not read God's intentions from the normal course of events any more than from the abnormal. Jesus' willingness to go to the cross for the sake of humanity was certainly not normal, and in that sense not natural, but Christians see in that act a peculiarly vivid revelation of God. Obviously, Thomists do not disagree. They hold that some acts are above and beyond the morality of natural law. What they oppose are acts that fall beneath it.

But what is the evidence that bringing an end to one's life is always to fall beneath the norm found in natural law? Most people, through most of their lives, do cling to life even against great odds and in the face of considerable misery. Indeed, living things in general do so. It is possible to draw the conclusion that this effort to maintain one's life is "natural" and also that acting according to nature is good. Does this mean that risking one's life for a cause falls below this norm? No, that is not asserted. Why, then, should it mean that choosing to die rather than to live on as a burden to ourselves and to others falls below the law of nature?

Perhaps most people cling to life even in this situation. But, surely, moral questions are not settled by statistics. In any case, it may be that more and more often those who have enjoyed not only their three score and ten years, but also four score and four score and ten, do not cling so strongly to life. Perhaps it is according to nature that at some point people are ready to die, and perhaps it is "against nature" to protract life beyond that point when health, or mind, has failed.

The Wider Context

The changed social and global context should also be an important factor in considering the importance of allowing those who want to die to do so. The ratio of the retired population to those who are working is growing. All predictions are that this ratio will continue to increase even if people work somewhat longer than in the past. The burden on the workers of supporting those who are no longer economically productive will grow. Meanwhile, it is also likely that an increasing segment of the retired population will require nursing care and other very expensive services over extended periods of time.

The United States has enormous economic resources, so it can be argued that this society can afford all that the aged need. However, the percentage of the population living in poverty is growing. This growth is not among the elderly, who have the votes to ensure that they are not denied support. It is among children. The continuing transfer of resources from children to the aged does not bode well for the future.

The implication is not that resources should be taken away from the elderly who want them and can use them for an enjoyable or productive life. That is not necessary, at least for the present. But when consideration of the cost of keeping those stricken with Alzheimer's disease alive and properly attended to is set in a wider social context, in which the needs of children are not being met, this cannot fail to affect judgments as to the social importance of allowing those who wish to die to do so.

Perhaps appropriate redistribution of resources would enable society to keep everyone alive with expensive medical and nursing care for a very long time without depriving children of the support they need. Even so, questions must be raised. The main question remains that of the rightness of keeping alive those who want to die. But there are other issues as well. The economic possibility of certain actions does not ensure that they are harmless to the environment. On the contrary, population times per capita consumption equals the impact on the environment. The per capita consumption of those who require a great deal of care is very high. A planet groaning under the pressures of the present level of consumption, especially of wealthy societies, cannot afford more. For the sake of the future, society should be looking for ways to reduce this pressure. Allowing more freedom of choice about life and death would be one way, less horrible than some alternatives, to do this.

Restrictions on the Right to Die

A major thesis of this book is that rights are never absolute. Certainly this applies to the right to die. The argument has been that the duty to live is not absolute, but that does not mean that it has no validity at all. For an individual to take her or his life with no regard for other considerations is not morally acceptable.

The right to die should be circumscribed in many ways. It could be required that a person wait thirty days after first expressing the intention before implementing it. It could be required that during that thirty-day period several responsible professionals not otherwise closely related to the person who wants to die interview her or him. The state could even require concurrence of a majority of these with the decision to die before it would be allowed. Perhaps these persons would also be required to talk with family members during this period in order to ascertain their feelings and judgments. If the conclusion should be negative, that is, that the person should not be allowed to terminate life, it should be necessary to attempt to devise ways of helping her or him through the crisis that precipitated the desire. Those who thwart another's project assume special responsibilities.

Obviously, laws of this sort would not prevent suicides that ignored all these requirements. No law can. Suicides have occurred throughout history, even when legal and ecclesiastical punishments were severe. But a situation in which it was generally known that society provided an acceptable procedure and that people were available with whom one's intentions could be discussed might actually inhibit some of the impulsive suicides now occurring. At any rate, these restrictions on the right to die should reduce the anxiety of those who fear that the loss of an absolute prohibition will have widespread negative consequences.

Thus new laws could support the right to die while expressing the general consensus of society that terminating one's own life is not a merely personal decision, that one's right to die is not absolute. They would make it possible for many people who long to do so to terminate their lives with dignity, with social approval, and with medical assistance. They would not signal that society no longer took the value of individual persons with utmost seriousness.

Those who fear that any relaxation of the prohibition will open the door to complex moral and legal questions are quite correct. For example, there will be times when the person whose life's termination is being considered is not able to take the lead in the discussion. There may be someone who has repeatedly stated, and perhaps put into writing, that he or she does not want to continue living if mentally incapacitated. The incapacitation may come suddenly, as the result of an accident or a stroke. At this point the injured or disabled person cannot make the request that will start the procedures leading toward death. Someone else must do this in the person's name, based on earlier statements. Whether the now-damaged person currently desires death may not be entirely clear. Furthermore, difficult judgments may be involved. The now-incapacitated person may have expressed a desire not to live unless there was some reasonable chance of recovering her or his faculties. But now that person cannot make the judgment as to whether such a chance is "reasonable." Someone else has to do so.

Society should help all its members to think about the array of possibilities in advance. Each person should put in writing her or his wishes, as many now do with respect to the use of extreme measures to keep them alive. Those who want to have their lives terminated under certain circumstances should say so. They should say to whom they wish to give the responsibility of making the decision when they are not able to do so themselves. Society can institute certain checks, but ordinarily the purpose would be to implement the desires of the person involved, as long as doing so does not inflict significant hardship on others.

Another difficult problem will arise with some patients who are in acute pain over a protracted period. The pain may be such that they prefer to die rather than endure it. Yet an observer, not immediately experiencing the pain, may view it in larger perspective, anticipating that at some point in the future a worthwhile life, free from unbearable pain, is likely. The sufferer judges that prospect insufficient reason to continue living now. The observer believes that the larger view does justify the endurance of the agony now. Who is correct? The sorts of safeguards here proposed would be likely to overrule the demand for death in many such cases, but not necessarily in all.

Other difficult questions will have to be dealt with someday as well. So far the argument of this chapter has been that those who desire to be kept alive as long as possible, regardless of costs and whatever their condition, have the right to this. However, the right to be kept alive as long as possible, especially when the life in question is quite meaningless, cannot be absolute. If keeping a human vegetable alive to satisfy a decision someone made years ago takes resources that are badly needed for fully human persons who could enjoy life themselves and make a contribution to others, then, at some point, the interests of society must outweigh the expressed preferences of the deteriorated person. Still, the expressed preferences should weigh heavily in the balance. Some wills are broken after the death of those who have made them, but the burden of proof lies on those who would violate the expressed desires of the deceased with respect to the distribution of their property. The situation should be similar here. The right to die should not be translated into a right to kill.

Probably, however, a change of ethos that led people to be reflective about the conditions under which they would want their lives terminated would reduce the number of those who think they want to have their bodies kept alive regardless of their mental and emotional condition. These would, in time, become sufficiently few that their wishes could be honored without excessive cost to the society as a whole. This approach would largely eliminate those legitimate anxieties raised by the idea of euthanasia that center on the possibility of one group of persons deciding questions of life and death for others. The answer should be, in virtually all cases, that people will make the decision about themselves, with social intervention only to reduce, not to increase, the likelihood of ending life.

These proposals cannot altogether allay the fears of those who believe that relaxing current taboos will lead to a dangerously changed ethos along lines discussed earlier in this chapter. No change is without its dangers. But the present situation is already actualizing the dangers that are implicit in a false absolutization of human life. Reform is urgent. The appeal to absolutes is an all-too-common ploy in defense of an intolerable status quo that is not factually or logically justified. Its consequences are horrendous. It is past time for a change.

Some readers may think that most of what this chapter asks for is already realized. Where people make clear their wishes to be allowed to die, most states allow doctors to withhold treatment that would keep them alive. Often doctors prescribe drugs for pain relief that also serve to shorten life. It is simply not the case that the medical profession does all it can to keep each body alive regardless of the wishes of those involved. And all of this has massive public support.

The illustration focused on in this chapter of the Alzheimer's patient, however, shows that the changes that have occurred so far do not get to the heart of the problem. Doctors do not have to adopt extreme measures to keep those suffering from this disease alive. Hence, merely withholding some treatment does not lead to death. There is no reason to sedate the patient in ways that speed the dying process. To implement the right of the victim of Alzheimer's disease to die with dignity requires positive action to cause death, and thus far there is great resistance to sanctioning such procedures legally or involving the medical profession in them.

But if one who is diagnosed as having this disease clearly and consistently expresses a preference to die rather than linger on for years in a decaying state, the argument of this chapter is that this person has the right to die. That implies that others have the duty to assist and that society has the duty to facilitate this process. Death with dignity requires that the acts can be public and approved and that the best wisdom of those who are best informed be at the service of those who need it.

For this to become possible, changes must occur in public opinion, in medical practice, and in law. They must occur also in theology and the church. Since the church still functions as a source of opposition to these changes, its first task is to repent. Beyond that, Christians have a special opportunity now to take the lead in providing a context in which people of all ages reflect together about their personal desires and express them in clear ways. Clergy can take the lead in supporting honest discussion and sharing of feelings about death and dying. Christian faith can be experienced in its real relevance to ultimately important questions in a way that has become rare when the church has discouraged consideration of these matters. A church that deals openly with matters of life and death can reclaim its rightful heritage as a community that speaks to those issues of greatest importance to all.

THREE

The Right to Live

————→✸←————

The Meaning of Being "Pro-Life"

The two preceding chapters, on the right to kill and the right to die, have also referred to the right to live. This right of human beings is much more firmly established in our culture, and it certainly deserves strong continuing support. Even if those who for good reasons wish to die have the right to do so, the emphasis should be that those who want to be kept alive despite loss of mental faculties have the right to live. They should make that desire known while they still can, and their wishes should be honored in all but the most extreme circumstances. They have the right to live. Certainly society should not relax any of the safeguards now exercised against the loss of life by those human beings who want to live.

Chapter 1 argued that authentic commitment to life should cross the boundaries separating human life from other forms of life. But the argument for this extension did not deny the right of human beings to kill other animals in many circumstances. Certainly the force of the argument was not to reduce human concern for human life. The purpose was to overcome the callousness this society exhibits toward the destruction of other living things.

Indeed, concern for human life should be heightened rather than diminished. Our First World society today too easily accepts killing of criminals of certain types and also in war. It seems to place the right to possess firearms ahead of the security of persons from random killing. It gives priority to high-tech ways of saving a few lives rather than to public health measures that would benefit far more. It often places economic gain above the security of life of human beings, especially those in the Third World. The basic need is to take more seriously the right to live!

Even more important than simply keeping people alive is reordering priorities so that those biologically capable of a full life can truly live. Simply preventing untimely death appears to be a very limited expression of being pro-life. Every child should be loved and cared for. Society should work to ensure that the child has a chance to become a full participant in the economy and in political life. Health care should be available to all, to ensure that physical and psychological suffering be minimized and the enjoyment of life maximized.

There are fundamental *theological* reasons for being pro-life. God is present in all living things. Indeed, God's presence *is* the life of all that lives. God *is* the life of the world. To live for God is to live in the service of life. That does not mean that one can avoid terminating the lives of other creatures. Life feeds on life. But people can live so as to minimize the cost to other living things and so as to respect them even when they must kill them. This cherishing of life applies *a fortiori* to those living beings who bear the *imago Dei*.

Today the label "pro-life" has been taken by those who focus their concern on one point, the right of every fertilized human ovum to become a human being. Many of those who commit themselves to this right also consistently support human life in all the other ways mentioned. Ronald J. Sider has written a book entitled *Completely Pro-Life*, with the subtitle *Building a Consistent Stance on Abortion, the Family, Nuclear Weapons, the Poor* (Downer's Grove, Ill.: Intervarsity Press, 1987). Evangelicals for Social Action set their opposition to abortion in the context of sensitive concern for the poor. The Catholic bishops have connected their stance in favor of the fetus with their opposition to nuclear war. The caricature of the pro-life movement as indifferent to other dimensions of human life is unjust to most of its proponents. The danger of narrowness exists in this movement, but then it exists in all movements of people who become deeply concerned about particular issues.

It may be a legitimate criticism, on the other hand, to say that the pro-life movement has been insensitive to the needs of all forms of life except the human. Even here there is an exception in David C. Thomasma, who is open to concern for animals as well. But in his book *Human Life in the Balance* (Louisville, Ky.: Westminster/John Knox Press, 1990) this openness comes as an afterthought that has little effect on the argument as a whole. It may also be a legitimate criticism to say that those who have labeled themselves pro-life have accented biological existence for human beings more than the quality of life. Also, some in the pro-life movement seem to neglect consideration of the rights of the mother, subordinating them altogether to the rights of the fetus. But all these criticisms should be made on a case-by-case basis rather than against all who support the right of the fetus to life.

It is important that the affirmation of human life, both in its commonality with all life and in its distinctiveness, be set in the widest context. It is also important that the quality of life and the rights of the mother be given full consideration in questions of abortion. But whatever criticism may be directed to the "pro-life" movement in these respects, its focus on the rights of the fetus, and even of the fertilized human ovum, has forced all Christians to attend to a very important question. For this Christians are in its debt.

The Historic Teaching of the Church

Many of the strongest opponents of abortion understand their position to be required by Christian faith, and they are correct that Christian opposition to abortion goes back to the early church. The issue then was not whether abortion was permissible but how serious an offense it was. All agreed that once the fetus possessed a human soul, feticide was murder. But one tradition, grounded in Aristotle and supported by Augustine and Aquinas, distinguished an early period of fetal life before it is formed by a human soul. This was often thought to last for forty days. During this period feticide was not murder and was, indeed, not a very serious offense. Augustine wrote: "The body is created before the soul. The embryo before it is endowed with a soul is *informatus*, and its destruction is to be punished with a fine. The embryo *formatus* is endowed with a soul. It is animate being. Its destruction is murder, and is to be punished with death" (*Questiones in exodum*, 80).

With so long a Christian tradition in opposition to abortion, many assume that there is a biblical basis for this rejection. In one sense there is. There are many biblical grounds for the affirmation of life, especially human life, and of the evil involved in destroying it. But even biblical scholars strongly opposed to abortion are forced to admit that there are no biblical prohibitions. (See T. C. Smith, "The Abortion Issue: A Biblical Perspective—A Baptist View," in *Seminar on Abortion*, edited by Claude U. Broach; Charlotte, N.C.: The Ecumenical Institute, 1975, p. 37.) Indeed, the only direct discussion of feticide in the Bible is Exodus 21:22–25. Here the feticide is accidental, and it is treated as the destruction of property to be compensated by a money payment.

It would be a mistake to argue from this general silence, or from this one passage, that the Hebrews, or Jesus, or Paul did *not* oppose all abortion. But it would be at least an equal error to claim any direct biblical authority against it. Today's strong opposition among many Christians is grounded in tradition, not Scripture. Within the tradition it sides with one group of authorities against another.

To say this is not to belittle the theological position that defends the fertilized human ovum as having full human rights. It is only to say that equally committed Christians can come to differing conclusions from study of the same traditional sources, and that both sides need further arguments. The U.S. Catholic bishops, for example, in defending the view that *human* life begins at conception, recognize this need. They appeal to empirical evidence (not available to Aristotle, Augustine, or Aquinas) to the effect that a great deal about the person-to-be is determined at conception and that "from fertilization the child is a complex, dynamic, rapidly growing individual" (*Documentation on the Right to Life and Abortion*, National Conference of Catholic Bishops; Washington, D.C.: United States Catholic Conference, 1974, p. 9). Their formulation may be exaggerated, but the evidence against a radical and abrupt change at some one point in the fetus's development, such as after forty days, is strong.

The Rights of the Fertilized Ovum

The chapters on the right to kill and the right to die argued that there is no basis for an *absolute* right to either life or death. All rights have to be seen in a larger perspective in which other rights are also considered. The real question is how the various rights are related to one another. There are conflicts in which it seems that one type of right always takes precedence over another. For example, the right of a person to a good night's sleep free from mosquito bites consistently takes precedence over the right of a female mosquito to live and to propagate her kind. But in other cases, even when the tension is between human rights and animal rights, the outcome is not so obvious. For example, it is by no means clear that the human right to eat tuna always takes precedence over the right of porpoises to live.

What about the right of a fertilized human ovum to live? It certainly has such a right. The question is how this right is to be related to other rights, such as the right of the mother to make her own decision about whether to take on the enormous responsibility involved in giving birth to a child, the right of the father to share in such a decision, the rights

of other children to have their interests considered, the right
of society to expand or contract its population, the right of
future generations to inherit a habitable world, the right
of other animals to be fruitful and multiply.

This way of putting matters is not common among the
strongly committed antiabortionists. Their tendency is to
view the right of the fertilized human ovum to life almost as
an absolute. This tendency is derived from two foundational assumptions: One, the fertilized human ovum is a
human being, so rights applying to human beings in general
apply to it; two, human beings, at least those innocent of
serious crimes, have an absolute, or near absolute, right to
life. The qualification "near" is needed in the case of those
who accept abortion if it is necessary in order to save the
mother's life.

Chapter 2 considered the second of these assumptions.
The notion of an absolute, or near absolute, right to life is
closely connected with the notion that human life is sacred.
But, biblically speaking, only God is sacred. Christians
should speak, instead, of God's unconditional love of all
creatures and especially of human ones. Christians should
also love unconditionally. This means that they should allow others to carry out their projects unless these are ex-
cessively harmful to themselves or to others. Love, then,
expresses itself foundationally not in keeping people alive
but in respecting their freedom and responsibility. Since the
great majority of people want to continue living and cannot
carry out their other projects without doing so, there is an
overwhelming weight in favor of keeping people alive. But
when a person clearly, and reasonably, expresses the desire
to terminate her or his life, this takes precedence. The person's right to have this desire respected, while not an absolute, does take precedence over the obligation to keep
people alive at all costs. Respect for the central projects of
others is called for by the unconditional love that is the
basis for Christian action.

In short, although the right of a human being to life is

quite fundamental, it is not absolute. It is derived from, and therefore subordinate to, the right of people to carry out their own projects. However, those to whom this right is properly attributed are those who have projects and can in some way express those projects.

When matters are approached in this way it is clear that the fertilized human ovum is not a proper object of the respect due to human beings simply because they are human. The respect due to the ovum cannot express itself as the support of its avowed projects. One may reasonably argue that the fertilized ovum has as its implicit project living and growing, and that proper respect for it should lead to support of that project. But this is true for the human fertilized ovum in no different sense than for that of a mouse. One cannot derive from that project the commitment to keeping the fertilized human ovum alive even at high costs to the mother and others, a commitment that is characteristic of the "right-to-life" movement.

This does not mean that there is no difference in the claim upon us of the human ovum as against that of the mouse. It does mean that the difference needs to be specified. The difference is that if the human fertilized ovum is allowed to live, it will become a human being, one who should be allowed to carry out her or his projects, and hence one who has a quite fundamental right to life. To prevent the emergence of this human being certainly involves a loss. What might have been will never be. A potentiality for a unique human life is lost forever.

From this it follows that there is a prima facie desirability that the fertilized ovum develop into a child. The language of rights, developed with matured human beings in view, is difficult to apply in this case. Instead of speaking of the right of the fertilized ovum, it might be better to speak of the right of society to be enriched by this additional member. But, however it is described, those concerned for the fertilized human ovum are not wrong in holding that its destruction is a real loss. This loss is to be seen primarily not in terms of what the ovum now already is but in terms of potentials that will never be actualized. An attitude of casual indifference is not warranted.

Those who argue for the "pro-choice" position focus on the situation of the pregnant woman, rather than on the ovum. On the other hand, somewhere in the development from fertilized ovum to baby, the focus shifts. Most agree that once the baby is born, the mother's choices should be ordered to the well-being of the child. Those who describe themselves as pro-life, on the other hand, focus on the fertilized ovum from the beginning. When chided for insensitivity to the well-being of the woman, some argue that Christians should be especially sensitive to the needs of the weak and powerless. The woman may be relatively weak and powerless in relation to other people, but in relation to the fertilized ovum she is immensely powerful. Hence these defenders of the rights of the fetus affirm that from the beginning it is the interests of the fertilized ovum that Christians should defend.

This argument has merit, although like so many others in this debate its full implications are rarely drawn. If weakness and powerlessness were the major considerations directing the concern of Christians, they would be far more attentive to the suffering they inflict on the other creatures with which they share this planet. But since Christians should become far more concerned about these other creatures, and should apply the principle far more consistently in dealing with other human beings as well, the pro-life movement should be supported on this point. Hence, without ignoring the interests of the mother or of others, discussion in this chapter of the right to life of an unwanted fertilized human ovum will continue with a focus of attention on the ovum.

It was stated above that if the fertilized human ovum were viewed only as such, as what it already is, its right to life would be hardly greater than that of the fertilized ovum of a mouse. That would count rather little when weighed against other rights that must be considered. On the other hand, when viewed in terms of what can come into being if life is not terminated, that is, a unique human being, there is something very precious here that deserves the respect of all. It is not foolish or misguided to defend that precious potentiality against arbitrary destruction. Still, the principle to which appeal should be made should not be the fundamental right of human beings to be supported in their project to live. This right is grounded in the existence of a human being who has a project that requires continued life for its completion. The fertilized ovum does not have that kind of project. The principle favoring the right of the ovum to life is, instead, that people should support the actualization of valuable potentials, especially the potential of becoming a human being. This principle cannot be construed as an absolute, but that does not make it unimportant.

What is properly objected to in the destruction of a fertilized ovum is the prevention of the development of a human being rather than the killing of one. The question now is how far the opposition to such prevention can be pushed.

Consider the situation in which a woman is ovulating and her husband is able to fertilize the ovum. A potential for a unique human being exists in that situation too. There is an ovum capable of being fertilized. There is a man with the sperm that can do the fertilizing. If the act of sexual intercourse needed to realize this potentiality is not performed, there is a loss—namely, the loss of some person who could have been brought into existence. The fact that the genetic character that person would have is not determinate can hardly be made the basis of a radical distinction between this and the case of the fertilized ovum where that determinateness exists. Yet most people, even the strongest advocates of the right of the fertilized ovum to life, do not call for the fertilization of as many ova as possible. Even those who oppose all artificial methods of birth control say nothing of the right of the ovum to be fertilized.

The absolute line they seem to draw between the right of

the fertilized ovum and the lack of right of an unfertilized one probably derives from a view that rights belong to human beings, that the unfertilized ovum is not a human being, and that the fertilized ovum is. But this formulation greatly exaggerates the differences. The change that takes place at the exact moment when fertilization occurs is important, but not absolute. In a very important and obvious sense, the unfertilized ovum is human. Its project, if one can speak of projects at this primitive level, is to be fertilized and to become a human being. In other very important senses, the fertilized ovum is not a human being.

Of course, fertilization is one necessary step in the process of development from an unfertilized ovum to a human being. But there are other necessary steps en route to becoming human. Far less confusion occurs if references to killing the ovum use just that language. Killing a fertilized ovum is *ovicide*, not murder! When the Roman Catholic bishops speak of the fertilized ovum as a "child," they distort the discussion, and when opponents of measures that prevent implantation of a fertilized ovum in the walls of the womb call this murder, their rhetoric makes reasonable discussion difficult. If an ovum is denied fertilization, it dies. If the fertilized ovum is denied certain conditions essential for its growth, it dies. In terms of what dies, there may be somewhat more value already realized in the fertilized ovum than in the unfertilized one. But in terms of the potential that will never be realized, the loss is much the same. A human being might have come into existence. That human being will never exist. The difference between failing to fertilize the ovum and preventing the fertilized ovum from being implanted is real, but not of overwhelming moral importance.

This discussion has begun by analysis of the extreme limit of the concern of the advocates of the right to life. The point is that they are not wrong in seeing something of great value and importance at stake. What is lost when the life of a fertilized ovum is terminated is the potentiality of a human being. This loss is essentially the same if an abortion is performed three months later. A similar loss also occurs when the opportunity to fertilize an ovum is passed up.

A Functioning Brain

By no means all of those who oppose abortion oppose the killing of fertilized ova. Many see the beginning of human life at later points. It is not practical to consider every possible place for drawing the line, but one other argument will be examined as an example: that of the philosopher Baruch Brody, whose study of the issues led him to switch from the easy acceptance of abortion to opposition. (See *Abortion and the Sanctity of Human Life: A Philosophical View*; Cambridge, Mass.: MIT Press, 1975.) The position to which he came is a contemporary version of the view of Aristotle, Augustine, and Thomas Aquinas mentioned earlier.

Brody sees that the first crucial issue is "essentialism." Those who reflect about humanity must affirm, he believes, that there is an essence of humanity, and that it is the presence of this essence in a being that calls forth the full respect that is to be accorded to any human being. Where this essence is absent, the entity in question is not human and does not warrant any special concern or treatment. Hence, like those who view the fertilized ovum as a human being, Brody believes that a definite line must be drawn, with full human rights accorded to everything that qualifies as human and none to what has not yet crossed that line. The difference is where the line is drawn.

Brody does not believe that the fertilized ovum has the essential characteristics of humanity. He argues that a functioning human brain is the essence of human being, so once such a brain emerges in the fetus, the fetus must be regarded as a fully human being. To kill a fetus with such a brain is for Brody morally the same as killing an adult human being.

Given that philosophical position, the question of when a

fetus becomes human must be a factual one, rather than a convenient stipulation for certain practical purposes. Brody judges that the "fetus becomes a human being sometime between the end of the second week and the end of the third month" (*Abortion and the Sanctity of Human Life*, p. 112). If this is so, then most abortions at least risk being murders.

The basic weakness of this approach is precisely the essentialism that is crucial to it and that Brody makes so explicit. From an essentialist perspective, there must be a line such that everything on one side of it is a human being and everything on the other side lacks any claim to special consideration. The preceding sections discussed the justification for drawing that line at the point of fertilization. Brody provides a second possibility: the emergence of a functioning brain. If a line must be drawn, these are certainly two possible and relatively plausible places to draw it. But there are a number of other equally reasonable candidates.

For example, it can be argued that conception has not really taken place until the fertilized ovum is implanted in the wall of the womb. In that case, preventing this step from taking place is birth control rather than abortion. Since there are standard procedures for preventing pregnancy that function in this way, and since even apart from such intervention nearly half of all fertilized ova fail to implant, the distinction between fertilization and implantation is an important one.

Alternately, the line may be drawn at viability. The question, it can be argued, is whether the life of the fetus is independent, or potentially independent, from the mother. Or it can be asserted that birth itself is the crucial line. Only with birth does the fetus become a baby and a member of the human community. It is even possible to argue that there is no real human being until some stage of maturation after birth. These days, in academic circles, the emphasis on language is so great that it may seem that one is not human until one participates in its use.

Once an essentialist mode of thinking is adopted, everything depends on the decision as to what constitutes the all-decisive essence. Such a decision, obviously, is highly disputable. There seems to be no basis on which agreement can be reached.

The truth is that something important happens at each of the points identified as possibilities for the drawing of a line, but that to turn one of the many necessary stages in the development of a human person into an absolute, and then to treat the others as negligible, is perverse. Is it not more consonant with good sense to recognize that there are a number of very important stages of human development, and that any answer to the question of when to say that the developing organism has become a human being is dependent on definitions of the human being that are somewhat arbitrary? If there must be a line, then it should be drawn for practical purposes as issues arise. It does not express a decisive fact about the objective humanity of the fetus itself.

Since the real issue is when to accord to the organism the sort of right to life that is accorded to mature members of the species, it would be well to ask what characteristics of mature human beings justify the ascription of this right. The point at which these characteristics emerge can then be ascertained. It is not the right to live in general that emerges at that point, for even the fertilized human ovum should be accorded some qualified right. The question is when the organism is to be accorded the nearly unqualified right to life of fully developed human beings.

From this point of view, the question is not whether a functioning human brain is essential to being truly human. Surely it is. The question is whether it is sufficient. The answer is, surely not. Being human has something to do with subjective experience. A functioning brain is certainly indispensable to that experience, but so are relationships with others. Whatever kind of experience the fetus has in the womb is very unlikely to have any of the distinctive characteristics that lead to attribution of special value and

importance to human beings in comparison with other animals. Indeed, the experience of a mature dog probably re-
sembles that of a mature human being more than does that
of a three-month fetus.

The implication is not that people should be more concerned about the mature dog than about the human fetus.
The implication is that the reason for prizing the human
fetus lies in its extraordinary potentiality, not in what it has
already become. A three-month fetus has already realized
many of the potentialities of the fertilized ovum, including
the potentiality of developing a functioning brain. But it is
the potentiality of that functioning brain to interact with
other people and the wider world, and thus to support genuinely human experience, that makes it so precious.

The Process of Becoming a Person

Although what is destroyed when a fetus with a functioning brain is killed is still primarily potentiality for becoming
a human being, nevertheless the actuality of what is killed is
far greater than in the case of a fertilized ovum. There is,
therefore, an important difference. Two major changes have
occurred. First, from a single fertilized cell there has developed a complex system of cells organized into organs and
united into a single organism. Second, within this organism
there has emerged a single centralized experience, related to
the brain and having a richness of experience quite beyond
that of any of the individual cells in the brain or elsewhere
in the body. It is reasonable to assume that the killing of
this more developed fetus involves pain of a sort an ovum
cannot feel.

These are major transformations en route to becoming a
human being. But there are additional transformations still
to come. Two are crucial to distinctively human experience.
First, the unified experiences related to, but not identical
with, the multiplicity of brain cells must develop a new kind
of sequential relation. An infant's experience is predomi-

nantly reflective of the condition of its body. When that bodily condition changes, there is little influence of its previous condition in its present experience. There is very little memory or anticipation. The infant lives quite fully in the present. This changes rapidly in early childhood. Although the present remains important, it is increasingly viewed and interpreted in a larger context that includes past and future. The child comes to have her or his own projects that demand respect. Experience becomes personal. That is, the relation of one momentary experience to the sequence of past experiences and to anticipated future ones has become more determinative than the immediate reception of bodily experience. For many animals this never happens, and life is lived quite fully in the present. But for human beings the present becomes the meeting place of past and future, largely shaped by memory and anticipation.

The second transformation is of the relation of the personal experience to the body. In infancy the function of the unified experience is to serve the body. The unified experience mediates between the physical condition of the body and the activities, such as crying, that are important for getting the attention the infant needs. But as time passes, the relation is reversed. Projects are envisaged and developed at the level of the unified experience. The body is used to implement these projects.

Although there are no neat lines distinguishing all human beings from all other animals by peculiarly human capacities, most other animals, at least in their natural condition, do not take this last step. They have unified experience with considerable memory and some anticipation. But this experience, even if it is called personal, is basically in the service of the body. The animal's projects are for the sake of the well-being of the body. Some animals do make great sacrifices for the sake of others, but it is hard to think of nonhuman animals sacrificing their bodily well-being for the sake of ideal goals. Yet this is widely characteristic of human beings. It is one way of thinking of the *imago Dei*.

These comments give some content to the notion that what is destroyed in the death of even a considerably developed fetus is not a human being in the sense in which human beings are the objects of exceptional duties and the subjects of special rights. It is a potential human being. It is now a potential human being with unified psychic existence and feelings and emotions. But these characteristics are shared with many animals whose right to life, in typical thought and practice, is quite conditional. It is still the potentiality rather than the actuality that grants special status.

The Mother's Perspective

The destruction of a highly developed fetus is without question a much greater evil than the destruction of a fertilized ovum. Not only is more lost, but there may be considerable suffering on the part of the fetus. Still, the most important difference between the older fetus and the fertilized ovum is not the extent to which the characteristics of human beings have been realized. It is rather the new pattern of relations between the fetus and human beings. In the case of the fertilized ovum, no one knows of its existence. No emotional attachment to it has been formed. Usually no one knows whether such an entity has been killed or not. What is lost is not mourned by others.

Once a woman becomes aware of a potential human being within her womb, this situation changes. Even if she does not want to bear a child, emotional ties begin to develop both to what the fetus already is and to the child that may be. Few women can be indifferent to either of these, and if such indifference is approximated, that can only be at some cost to the personality of the mother. If others share the knowledge, the pattern of relations is richer. The longer these relations exist, the greater is the loss and suffering if, for whatever reason, the fetus dies. If it dies because of the woman's decision, the pain is greater still. Sometimes the pain is so protracted that women in later years regret having decided upon an abortion, however acute the hardships avoided.

This is a very different argument against abortion than the one based on the rights of the potential human being. But in the present context, they are not unconnected. The major reason for the woman's suffering in the death of the fetus is simply natural. It has been argued that women are so constituted that tender concern for the new life within them is biologically and psychologically natural. But there is a secondary reason, stemming from social teaching. As long as many people believe and teach that feticide is a terrible sin, grief is compounded with guilt. Even conscious disagreement does not protect one. At this point, a change in social ethos could reduce the suffering of the mother in making the decision for an abortion. The right-to-life movement is, among other things, an effort to prevent that kind of change from taking place. The movement is correct in affirming that it is wrong to treat feticide as morally indifferent. But the real problem is excessive feelings of guilt when the decision to abort is otherwise justified. In any case, no change in ethos would completely end this suffering.

The major reason for supporting early abortions and opposing later ones is not, then, that what is destroyed is of greater value in itself or more subject to suffering, although this is true. The major reason is that the shorter the period in which the woman forms attachments to the fetus, the less she will suffer in terminating its life. This is a very significant point. Once the woman thinks of the fetus as a baby, the emotions that are natural and appropriate toward a baby come into being. The violation of those maternal feelings is likely to do permanent damage. In some cases, even if the woman thinks she wants an abortion, others, with a wider knowledge of human psychology, should work against it.

The focus of discussion has now shifted from the potential human being to the actual woman. This leads to support of "freedom of choice." Respecting human beings means supporting their right to realize their own projects. The woman's projects should be supported out of respect for her right to choose. But this right, like all rights, is relative. The previous chapter argued that if one's choice to die adversely affects others, then one's right is qualified. Others have the right and duty to share in the decision. They may have an understanding of the situation that, in the intensity of immediate feelings, the one contemplating suicide cannot match. "Freedom of choice" is too strong an expression to apply when choices affect others as well as the chooser.

In the case of the decision to abort, there are always negative consequences. These include the death of the potential human being. That is a serious matter, but it is not decisive by itself. To kill the newly fertilized cell is little worse than to prevent fertilization. It can be considered a legitimate extension of birth control.

When the fetus has developed many of the physical features of human beings and has begun to have its own unified experience, what is destroyed in feticide is of quite considerable value in itself, even if it is not yet a full human being. Further, the woman will have developed an attachment to the fetus in her womb, the violation of which has extensive negative repercussions for her. Others are also likely to be involved by this time. To counterbalance all of this, the reasons for an abortion must be weighty.

Much thought has been given to what may constitute such weighty reasons. Knowledge that the fetus cannot develop into a normal child can constitute such a reason. The fact that the fetus is the result of rape can be another. The mother's mental or physical health is a third. But there are many more, and any effort to list them falsifies the actual process of decision-making that must go on in the agony of each individual case.

By the time a woman knows there is new life within her, the value of that life in itself and her emotional attachment to it have become significant factors. The attachment increases as the fetus grows and becomes more active. If there are good reasons for abortion, the feticide should occur as early as possible. Yet the decision should not be that of the woman alone. Perhaps a week's delay, during which time professional counseling is provided by society, should be required. On the whole, counseling should be directed toward helping the woman make her own decision, but in extreme cases it may be appropriate for a counselor to have the authority to prevent the abortion or to carry the case to someone who does. If the desire of the woman for an abortion is countermanded, then society must assume major responsibility to help her deal with the crises she foresees.

These conclusions have supported the primacy, though not the exclusiveness, of the right of the woman to decide and the undesirability of establishing rules indifferent to her situation. But at some point the woman's rights cease to be determinative. No one believes a mother has the right to kill her two-year-old child, however great the hardship imposed on her by the child's existence.

Despite the lack of any one change in fetal-infant development that justifies drawing a line between rightless nonhumanness and the possession of full human rights, for practical purposes a line must be drawn with respect to any specific right. In this case the issue is the right to life. If it is recognized for what it is, a partly arbitrary social decision, then laws following from drawing the line can be enforced with some flexibility.

At least superficially, the clearest line is birth itself. Whereas many ancient societies practiced exposure of unwanted infants, Christians overwhelmingly rejected this practice, and this rejection has now become general throughout the world. From this consensus it is a small step to the view that premature infants should have the same protection as others, if by such protection they can be kept alive—in short, if they are viable. This remains true even if the fetus has been artificially removed from the womb. Hence, viability constitutes a natural and widely accepted boundary. Once a fetus is viable, reasons for killing it should be very weighty indeed.

The prohibition, or severe restriction, of killing a viable fetus has considerable support in society as a whole. For practical purposes this works well today in virtually excluding abortions after twenty-three or twenty-four weeks of gestation. Insofar as a line must, for legal purposes, be drawn, this seems to be the best place to draw it.

One concern about drawing a line this way is that to some extent viability is a function of medical science and technology. As these advance, younger fetuses can be kept alive. This accents the point that there is no drastic change in the fetus at some one point. In principle, technological ability might lower the age of "viability" considerably. Indeed, someday it might be possible to fertilize an ovum outside the womb and provide an artificial environment. In some sense the unfertilized ovum would then already be "viable."

Despite such reductions of the criterion to absurdity, for the foreseeable future it can work reasonably well. During the past fifteen years the age at which a fetus can be kept alive with artificial aid has been lowered less than fourteen days, and the danger that these younger fetuses will not develop into healthy infants is considerable. Assuming that "viability" includes a reasonable chance to develop into a normal human being, there is no reason to expect major changes soon.

It should also be emphasized that the right to life of the viable fetus remains relative. If the mother's life is endangered, few hesitate to save her at the expense of the fetus.

The Wider Context

A consistent theme in this book is that a purely individualistic view of rights should be rejected. Human lives are so bound together that all decisions about life and death need to involve the others who are affected. This is true even when only the well-being of those most closely involved is considered. But, in fact, changes in attitudes toward life and death are important for the whole community, indeed, for all humanity. Hence the issue should be viewed also with a much wider horizon.

One context in which the discussion of abortion now needs to be set is that of the recent realization of the depth and comprehensiveness of the oppression of women in patriarchal society. The question of whether a woman should bear a child has in the past been decided, for the most part, in terms of the interests of men, and the woman's role has been to serve the patriarchal society. This is not the place to elaborate on the extensive denial to women of control even over their own bodies. There is justice in the current demand on the part of women that their right to decide about what happens in their bodies be respected. Because self-determination is so central to women's struggles today, this right should be given special weight.

Some women today, in reaction to millenia-long deprivation of rights, use absolutistic language about this right to determine their own destinies and to control what happens in their own bodies. Some have overstated the extent to which the fetus is part of their bodies and lacking in independent existence and value. This exaggeration is an almost necessary reaction to the continuing tendency in a patriarchal society to subordinate women's rights to those of others—the father on the one side, and the fetus on the other.

Given the historic context of the discussion today, there is reason to lean heavily toward the affirmation of the woman's right to decide. Society has the duty to lean over backward to assist women who are seeking, psychologically and publicly, to take full responsibility for their lives. The decision as to whether to bear or not to bear a child is so central to that responsibility that social interference should be muted.

The proposals made above about mandatory delay and counseling before an abortion are in tension with the demands of some women for complete control over the decision. Such tensions are the stuff of both morality and politics. The tension cannot be removed, but it can be eased if the implementation of such proposals is sensitive to the massive oppression that women have suffered and continue to suffer. For example, any required counseling or, in the extreme case, any decision to refuse the woman's request, should be by women who are themselves committed to the empowering of women.

There is also a still wider context within which this reflection needs to proceed. The historic opposition to abortion arose in general in societies where it was in the interest of the community to have more children. Where so many children died in the early years, the prevention of a potential birth was antisocial. It threatened the survival of the community as a whole. All the traditional religions came into being in that kind of world. Marrying, having children, and bringing them to adulthood so that they in their turn would marry and have children was foundational to the individual's responsibility to society. If that were the situation today, then, although the personal needs of the pregnant woman might sometimes outweigh the interest of society in having more children, her reasons to abort even a very young fetus would have to be quite strong.

But this is not the kind of world in which we live. On the contrary, overpopulation is a major problem. Indeed, it contributes to many deaths, especially of children, through hunger and malnutrition. These are closely related to other problems, such as resource exhaustion, pollution, climate change, depletion of the ozone layer, desertification, deforestation, and erosion, that make the prospects of the newborn bleak. Overpopulation is connected with problems of social injustice and war as well. Population stabilization is a high priority for any rational social policy in most countries. In time the issue may become how to reduce population humanely.

For the world as a whole, therefore, it is generally desirable that the rate of births be reduced. Given that fact, it seems evident that it is better for this reduction to come from unwanted births rather than from wanted ones. The time may come when more countries limit the right of couples to have even the children they want. That will be a sad day! But because that may become necessary for the sake of preserving the possibility of a decent life for future generations, it is certainly desirable now to seek ways of stabilizing population that do not involve this denial of freedom to propagate as one chooses. Giving women now the right *not* to have children, the right *not* to bring fertilized ova to term, is certainly one of the more favorable ways of attaining the goal. It implements the general principle that unconditional respect for others expresses itself in allowing them to fulfill their projects. If society now grants the right not to have unwanted children, it may assure future couples the right to have wanted ones. Neither of these rights is absolute, but both should be real.

This reference to the wider context is usually omitted in the consideration of issues that are thought to belong to personal ethics. Indeed, many view this qualification of the autonomy of personal ethics with horror. It seems to imply that social needs can override individual rights, and this seems to be precisely the doctrine of totalitarianism against which Christians have struggled so hard. There is much justification for this concern.

However, the effort to dissociate individual matters from social ones is unrealistic. The evil of totalitarianism arises from its tendency to treat the collective as if it had some kind of existence and value apart from the persons who make it up. The interests of the "fatherland" could be conceived of in ways that were clearly not the interests of the people who lived in, and constituted, the nation. This hypostatization of the nation must be vigorously opposed. But extreme individualism is little better. To accent the rights of individuals and the freedom of individuals in ways that cause all to suffer together does not really serve the individuals. Individuals exist as part of the community, and the community is nothing more than its members in their mutual relationships.

Garrett Hardin's parable of the commons is telling here. Hardin describes a pasture open to all herdsmen. Each herdsman gains by adding cattle to the commons. Up to a certain number, his gain costs the others nothing. But even beyond that number, even when the grazing exceeds the carrying capacity of the commons, adding an animal still benefits the individual herdsman, since the gains are his, while the costs are shared by all. Hence, when each pursues his own interest rationally, the commons are destroyed, and all lose. (*Exploring New Ethics for Survival: The Voyage of the Spaceship Beagle*; New York: Penguin Books, 1972, p. 254.)

If each individual is free to use shared resources without check, all will suffer through their overuse. All benefit if the total use is within the carrying capacity of the system. Once population passes a certain point, the task is not to guard the freedom of each individual to do as she or he pleases, but to establish as just a system of distributing the rights to use the resources as can be devised. If population reaches the limit of the carrying capacity of human beings living at an acceptable level of resource use, then the right to reproduce can no longer be viewed as absolute. A decision that was previously made by each couple privately now becomes a matter of public importance. All will suffer if human population continues to rise. Individual rights must be adjusted to the new situation.

Drastic action is not needed in the United States, at least for the present. Such action was needed in China and is needed in some other places. Still, even for the United States now, consideration of the respective rights of fetus and mother needs to be set in this larger context. If society's interest lay in the woman's giving birth to every fertilized ovum in her womb, that should count in the balance. If society's interest is in reducing the number of births, and especially of unwanted ones, then this should count in the balance also.

The lives of the members of the community are bound together. It is in the community's interest that its members have as much freedom as possible in making decisions about their own lives. But if those decisions imperil the community, that means that they imperil all the individuals who make up the community. It is in the interest of all these individuals that the community restrain actions by each that thus imperil all. The aim should be to devise policies that maximize both personal freedom and community well-being.

This book is proposing such policies. The right to die should be granted to those aged people for whom life ceases to have positive value either to themselves or to others and who desire to die. The right to end an unwanted pregnancy, especially at an early stage, should be granted to women. Such rights are not absolute. They should be checked by society. Both the decision to terminate a severely deteriorated life and the decision to prevent a potential human being from actualizing that potentiality are serious ones that involve loss and suffering. Nevertheless, they are often justified by immediate considerations without regard to the wider context. When that context is fully considered, the importance for society to grant that right to those most closely involved is accentuated.

Granting the right to individuals to have more control over their own lives is in itself a humane action. This humane action will ease problems of population growth. If society fails to take humane measures of this sort now, the next generation may be forced to take inhumane actions. Christians do not have the right to impose on the future the kind of world that allows their children no other choices.

FOUR

The Right to Love

———→✠←———

Current Protestant Views of Sexuality

The topic of this chapter is not love in general; it is sexual love. Without that emphasis, the topic would be noncontroversial, at least in Christian contexts. No one challenges the right of anyone to love others in a variety of important senses of that term. Even with respect to sexual love, there is less controversy on some aspects than there once was. Most Christians acknowledge that humans are sexual beings, and that the desire for sexual contact with others is natural and inevitable. Difficulties arise with respect to the right to act on that desire before marriage, and the most intense controversy rages today around homosexual acts. Hence, the two main questions to be addressed are: Do heterosexuals have the right to engage in sexual intercourse before marriage; and, Do homosexuals have the right to act out their sexuality at all?

The sexual revolution has led many to treat the right to express sexual desire, whether heterosexual or homosexual, as almost absolute. The "almost" is needed, since few believe they have the right to force others to submit to their desires, and most place limits on relations with children, even if the children are, in some sense, willing. But sexual activities between or among consenting adults are affirmed with few or no qualifications. The right to love, in this specific sense of love, is strongly affirmed by those who have most fully internalized the sexual revolution. This forthright affirmation challenges Christians to clarify their convictions.

The revolution was initially against a social view that sex in general is unclean, at best a necessary evil to be restricted as much as possible. Roman Catholics long continued to see the life of those who renounced sexual intercourse as superior to others, while teaching that the only justification of sexual intercourse is procreation. This served to limit acceptable sexual intercourse to marriage. The recent abandonment of this view by Catholics, at least in the North Atlantic countries, has contributed in a major way to the decline in religious vocations.

Protestants rejected the claim that the celibate life is a superior one, and developed a more positive and varied view of marriage. But they did not uproot, indeed, they hardly challenged, the sense of uncleanness connected with sex. Even today a joke is called "dirty" if it deals with sex. It was the sexual revolution, coming from outside the church, and often as an attack on the church's teaching, that gradually forced Christians to rediscover the more wholesome view of sexuality in the Bible.

Most Christians today, thanks to the sexual revolution, have recovered the biblical affirmation of sexuality in general, and of the physical pleasure of sexual intercourse in particular, as gifts of God. This is a profoundly positive change. But most Christians still find unacceptable the almost unqualified affirmation of the "right to love" coming from the more thoroughgoing supporters of the sexual revolution. Christians today refuse to choose between sex as unclean on the one side and the right to unrestricted sexual expression on the other. The resultant task is to find convincing norms or guidelines for sexual conduct, as for all forms of conduct.

Despite this gain in the affirmation of sexuality, much Christian discussion of sexual activity is still couched in moralistic terms. One asks whether a particular sexual activity is wrong. The implication is that if it is not forbidden, then there is no further moral question.

An authentically Christian approach is quite different. For

example, the issue is not whether adolescent sexual play violates a moral law. The question is, What is the best way to order adolescent sexual life to the larger ends to which God calls? The answer cannot be the same for every adolescent at all times and places, but some generalizations are nevertheless possible.

When Christians reflect on what is best in the sexual area of life, two principles operate that have been absent, or at least muted, among those who have most fully imbibed the spirit of the sexual revolution. First, although sexuality is a good, it is a limited good. A limited good treated as a final good becomes an idol. Sexual fulfillment as an end in itself, separated from other concerns, becomes idolatrous and, therefore, demonic. Second, all of life is lived in the context of a wider community. Hence, the best decisions will take into account their place in the pattern of relations that constitute that wider community, and they will express the mutual responsibility that sustains the community.

The pattern of sexual life most often held by Protestants to be ideal is that of monogamous marriage in which both partners come to the marriage bed as virgins. This model has much to commend it. Its embodiment contributes to the intimacy and security of marriage. It provides a healthy context for children. It settles many questions in ways that allow energies to be devoted to serving God more fully. It contributes to the building of community between the families of the two partners. For those who genuinely internalize this ideal, it is not repressive, although it requires discipline no less demanding than that required to attain excellence in athletics or music.

Nevertheless, most Protestants have found it necessary to modify this ideal in order to relate it effectively to the actual world. Divorce, which was once forbidden as contradictory to the ideal, is now recognized as often being the best solution to problems that arise in attempting to realize it. This is because the ideal has itself evolved. Whereas in the past the maintenance of a marriage was virtually an end in itself, or was seen as essential for the propagation and raising of children and the transmission of property, now it is understood first and foremost as a means to the fulfillment of the partners. When it fails in this respect, divorce with all its trauma is often affirmed as preferable to the continuation of the marriage.

Furthermore, most Protestants affirm remarriage as often, indeed usually, a positive step after divorce. Of course, they hope that the new marriage will be permanent and that it will come closer to fulfilling the new ideal of marriage. They certainly commend fidelity within it. The point is only that in the choice between limiting sexual intercourse to a single partner throughout life and a reasonable chance for the happiness of the people involved, most Protestants now opt for the latter.

Protestants are becoming so accustomed to this acceptance of divorce and remarriage as the best response in many circumstances, that they might forget how drastic a change this is from past Christian teaching if Catholic unwillingness to accept divorce did not repeatedly remind them. This change among Protestants is particularly noteworthy since it is the acceptance of a practice that is rejected explicitly in the Bible. Further, the prohibition appears at a far more central place than is the case with other doctrines on which many Protestants continue to appeal to Scripture as authoritative. It is Jesus himself who opposed divorce!

The conclusion to be drawn is not that Protestants should go back to a legalistic prohibition of divorce. On the contrary, they have been far more faithful to Jesus as they have become concerned to relieve suffering and give people a second chance than have those who do legalistically adhere to Jesus' declaration. The point, instead, is that if many Protestants are prepared to make this move, they should be open to reconsidering, on similar grounds, other aspects of the church's traditional teaching as well.

Premarital Sexuality

One important focus of this reconsideration should be the period of adolescence and early adulthood. This is the time in which, in many traditional societies, marriage typically occurred, often early enough, at least for the woman, so that most sexual maturation took place within marriage. Now society requires a long delay. Further, whereas in an earlier day intercourse was hardly separable from the prospect of pregnancy and sometimes from the danger of disease as well, today precautions can be taken that allow the enjoyment of sexuality with much less anxiety about such consequences.

Hence, now when the church says to young people, "Just say no," it often does so without giving convincing reasons for this abstinence. To those who decide that they will not obey this apparently arbitrary rule, the church gives little guidance in sorting out the actual complexities and difficulties that are involved in adolescent sexual activity. The church's contribution is only to declare that all their sexual intercourse is wrong. It makes no distinctions. Adolescents are left to work out their own codes and expectations without much help from adults in general, and with almost none from the church. The result is often self-destructive. The church can then point to the negative consequences of premature and irresponsible sex and say, "We told you so." Surely the church can do better than this!

Christian reflection about sexuality before marriage will be irrelevant and inappropriate unless it keeps in mind the changes that have come about since the time when the traditional Christian ideal was formed. Five of these have been mentioned in passing.

First, there is the postponement of the time of marriage, especially for women. Today a longer period of education is expected, and in general adolescent marriages are discouraged. Since it is women upon whom, traditionally, the ideal of chastity before marriage has been most strongly impressed, this change is a very important one.

Second, sexual intercourse is now affirmed as intrinsically good and enjoyable rather than being viewed with suspicion as a necessary evil. Hence, it is intrinsically good experience that young people are asked to forgo.

Third, sexual activity before marriage can be largely free from the danger of pregnancy and disease. Of course, pregnancy and disease are still serious problems, but they result from failure to take available precautions more than from inescapable risk.

Fourth, the purpose of marriage has changed from a primary focus on property and procreation to a primary focus on mutual support and fulfillment of the partners. Thus mutual faithfulness until death is for the sake of this support and fulfillment and not an end in itself or tied to property rights.

Fifth, in Protestant circles as in the wider society, divorce and remarriage are accepted. Indeed, they have become very common, so that the expectation that a marriage will endure until the death of one partner is greatly reduced.

Four other changes are equally important.

First, the extension of the period between sexual maturation and marriage is due not only to the postponement of marriage, but also to earlier biological maturation, at least in the North Atlantic world. According to a recent estimate, "For each generation since 1850 . . . a girl's period has come about a year earlier than her mother's" (Janice Delaney, Mary Jane Lupton, and Emily Toth, *The Curse: A Cultural History of Menstruation*, revised edition; Champaign, Ill.: University of Illinois Press, 1988, p. 49).

Second, the ideology of individualism, developed in the eighteenth century, has shaped the reality of twentieth century life to such an extent that the practical meaning of subordinating personal fulfillment to community is often obscure.

Third, this ideology has worked its way out in social institutions so as to undermine stable communities in general and extended families in particular. Peer approval is now more important to most adolescents than relations with adults. As a result, the expectations of the latter often are felt as oppressive.

Fourth, the liberation of women has so changed their situation that no dual standard of female virginity and male experimentation can make sense. There can be no return to the pattern that was in fact accepted by the church through much of its history.

Given this quite new situation, there are three basic options. One is to *maintain* the church's teaching intact, supporting it on legalistic and authoritarian grounds. The second is to *revitalize* the traditional ideal in the new context, so that it can be internalized and lived joyfully by serious Christian youth. The third is to *develop new models* of responsible Christian sexuality for young people.

The first option needs only to be stated clearly to be shown as inadequate. The declaration that sexual intercourse before marriage is morally wrong could earlier be supported by depicting sexuality itself as something negative, by emphasizing the danger of pregnancy and disease as punishments here and now and the prospect of hellfire beyond death, or by appealing to knowledge of God's will embodied in the church or in the Bible that a mere youth was in no position to question. None of this works well today. Further, when it does work, it damages the youth who live under this legalism. Indeed, this style of argumentation is contrary to the Christian gospel itself. Instead of freeing people to mature responsibility, it imposes unintelligible and arbitrary rules on the basis of heteronomous authority. In short, this kind of argument is far more clearly at odds with Christian faith than is the conduct it seeks to inhibit.

The second option aims at the same result by authentically Christian means. It affirms that there is an ideal expression of human sexuality such that its attainment is worthy of extensive sacrifice. It recognizes that this sacrifice has increased greatly in modern society, but it still claims that even this larger sacrifice is warranted by the good that is to be attained. Living in terms of the ideal is held to maximize the fulfillment of both partners in a context that also builds up the wider community and allows all concerned to order their lives to the service of God.

To argue that the postponement of sexual intercourse until marriage is necessary or even desirable for the fulfillment of this ideal involves two major steps. First, a mutually faithful marriage itself must be shown to realize the values claimed for it or at least to be more likely to do so than any other pattern of sexual relations. Second, it must be shown that this kind of marriage is possible only when sexual intercourse is postponed until marriage or, at least, that it is significantly more likely to occur under these circumstances.

Both steps in this argument are difficult to demonstrate convincingly in our present situation. First, the changed ideal of marriage that renders it more attractive, that is, the mutual support and fulfillment to which it is ordered, relativizes the limitation of sex to one partner throughout life. When a marriage ceases to fulfill the needs of the partners, the primary argument in its favor seems to turn against it. If this were a rare occurrence, the ideal could remain intact as an ideal. But when a high percentage of marriages fail, even a majority, then the idealization of one marriage as the only context of sexual expression itself becomes problematic.

To whatever extent the failure of marriages can be attributed to sexual infidelity, the ideal of faithful marriage can be sustained. And there is no doubt that infidelity is an important factor in marital failure and divorce. More disciplined sexual commitment would save many marriages. But this fact does not resolve the dilemma. Marriages also fail when the partners are sexually faithful to each other. Sometimes they fail precisely because expectations of fulfillment through a single relationship are unrealistically high, and mutual commitments are allowed to block other needs. Sometimes they fail because the patriarchal elements so pervasive of marriage block the liberation of the woman. Today we are learning a great deal about unhealthy patterns of codependency that have often been part of the very ideal of marriage. In view of all this, and much else that could be said, the traditional ideal requires, at a minimum, much clarification and re-envisaging before it can have great power with youth.

Even if this first step can be made convincing, there remains the second. Is it the case that sexual activity before marriage, either with other partners or between those who later marry, significantly reduces the likelihood of a successful marriage? Here the evidence is at best mixed. It is not possible to make a strong case against premarital sexual intercourse on this basis. Those who try to do so will understandably be suspected of rationalizing prejudices rather than reporting facts.

The traditional Christian ideal remains a beautiful one. It should not be set aside. Many of us older Christians are glad that we grew up in a context in which we were encouraged to live by it, and where the pressures not to do so were far less than they are today. But it is not the only ideal by which Christians can and should guide their sexual conduct. It is time to consider the third option seriously and openly.

I suggest that the church should survey what is actually going on among those who have not been convinced that sexual abstinence until marriage is desirable. Within this scene, Christians can certainly distinguish healthier and less healthy patterns. Rather than condemning them all equally, Christians should use their influence to support the healthiest and most responsible forms of sexual activity that they discern and to discourage others.

The best and healthiest patterns that have developed appear to be relatively long-term pairings in which a young man and a young woman live together and support each other while being sexually faithful. Much of what Christians hope for in marriage is often realized in these pairings. Indeed, since some of them last longer than some marriages, they are not always easy to distinguish from marriage in substantive ways.

Nevertheless, there are differences. A marriage embodies the intention of permanence and public affirmation. These may be desired for many reasons. One or both partners may want the additional security in the relationship provided by this mutual commitment and official sanction. Often there are other motivations. Temporary pairings do not encourage the families of the partners to develop serious relationships, as marriage does. And they are not an adequate context for raising children. Often it is the decision to have a child that precipitates the marriage of a couple who have been living together contentedly for some time.

In many earlier societies people thought youth were ready for marriage at least by seventeen or eighteen. Today we expect them to wait. There are good reasons for believing that few youth are ready to make lifelong commitments or to take on the responsibilities of caring for children in our society at that young age. But perhaps they are ready to find partners with whom they can share themselves in many ways, including sexually. Perhaps the church needs to recognize this and sanction such pairings whose purpose is mutual support and love and not childbearing, and where the duration of the relationship is left open. Property need not be mutually committed. There will be pain when such bondings are broken, but because children and property are not involved, and because no permanent commitments are entailed, these partings need not have the ramifications of divorce. Pairing with different partners will be accepted until such time as one is ready for a permanent commitment, in the context of which children may be brought into the world and cared for and which will bond the families as well.

This is essentially the proposal of Bishop John Shelby Spong, that the church sanction what he calls "betrothals" (John Shelby Spong, *Living in Sin?* San Francisco: Harper & Row, 1988, pp. 177–187). If a pattern of this sort were affirmed by the church as, at least, next best to its ideal, continued opposition to sexual intercourse outside of committed relationships might make sense to far more people.

To ask youth to wait until they are seventeen or eighteen makes more sense than to ask them to wait until a marriage that may not occur until they are twenty-eight. It is also possible that youth who have understood the whole of their sexual activity to be tied to responsible commitment will both better understand what is involved in marriage and better realize its ideal of permanence than have many Christians of today's adult generations.

The usual opposition to such proposals is that they give the church's sanction to fornication, and that this is one of the sins on Paul's list. But the Greek word *porneia*, often translated *fornication*, does not refer primarily to sexual intercourse between persons who are not married. Indeed, it may not refer to this at all! (Bruce Malina, "Does *Porneia* Mean Fornication?", *Novum Testamentum* XIV (1972), pp. 10–17.) The clearest and primary reference in general is to cult prostitution. In the one Pauline passage where the context determines the meaning (1 Cor. 5–6), the reference is to incest. Probably *porneia* often means illicit sexual practice as that is defined in the Torah and especially in Leviticus. But there sexual intercourse between unmarried, consenting adults is not specified for rejection.

This does not, of course, establish that Paul approved of what is called fornication today. Paul believed that self-indulgence in general was to be avoided, and irresponsible sexual intercourse would be a form of such self-indulgence. We are closer to Paul in opposing irresponsible sexual intercourse in general than in singling out what we call fornication for condemnation. In fact, Bishop Spong's proposal implements Paul's opposition to *porneia* more than it violates it. In Paul's day the denial to oneself of all sexual intercourse prior to marriage was not, for most people, anything like the sacrifice it is today. The effort now to introduce responsibility into sexual relations during late adolescence and early adulthood is not a violation of his moral teaching nor is it in opposition to the spirit of that teaching.

Another source of opposition comes from those who are particularly eager that the church maintain its integrity untarnished by the changing attitudes and practices in the society around it. They argue that any modification of church teaching to accommodate changing sexual mores is unacceptable compromise. This criticism deserves to be taken very seriously. Nothing is more important for the church today than to develop its own ethos, one truly continuous with its heritage and faithful to Jesus Christ. For it simply to sanction the dominant ideas and practices of its time for the sake of gaining members and social acceptance is a profound betrayal of its calling. In opposition to such compromise, groups like the Sojourners model consistent faithfulness in moving and convincing ways.

What is impressive about the Sojourners, however, is not legalistic maintenance of past church practices so much as radical reconsideration of all features of the tradition in light of what it means truly to embody the gospel today. The Sojourners have found, in identification with and service among the poorest of the poor in Washington, D.C., a form of witness that seems truly appropriate in our time and place.

But would an analogous attempt to reshape sexual life according to New Testament patterns make sense? That could lead to much earlier marriages, arranged by the family. Perhaps someday that will seem preferable to the present chaos, but surely we should not adopt this system simply because it was widely practiced in New Testament times. Or it could lead to affirmation of lifelong celibacy as the preferred pattern, and accepting new marriages only as a concession to human weakness. This has some support from both Jesus and Paul. It made sense when the end of the age was expected imminently, but most Christians, and especially most Protestants, agree that the transplantation of these norms in other contexts is a dubious strategy.

The church has long known that it cannot and should not follow the New Testament pattern in any such literal fashion in this important area, and it has developed teachings that have no direct support in the Bible. For example, the Protestant idealization of marriage certainly does not follow New Testament teaching in any straightforward way. Protestants should be as free to adapt New Testament teaching to today's situation as the Reformers were to adapt it to theirs.

Despite continued institutional and official opposition from the church, many, perhaps most, Christian parents have accepted sexual practices on the part of their children along the lines of commitment described. Most preachers in the old-line Protestant churches have refrained from denouncing these practices, and have married couples who have been living together without trying to make them feel guilty for the lifestyle they have chosen. Thus in some respects the church has already acquiesced in much of the program here proposed. The move now needed is from passive acquiescence that does not discriminate between promiscuity and faithful pairing to critical affirmation of the finest models.

Homosexuality

But there is another segment of society whose sexual explorations have not been so readily accepted. I refer to those whose sexual desires are directed to persons of their own sex. Millions of parents who are quite content for their children to be living in heterosexual partnerships, even when they are not sanctioned by marriage, would be shocked and appalled if they found that the partners were of the same sex.

There are many reasons for this shock. First, most people in this society, even those with homosexual inclinations, are "homophobic." That is, their self-understanding as sexual beings is challenged and disturbed by the encounter with homosexuality, both in themselves and in others, and they react with fear. This is true of many Christian parents. But even if homophobia is overcome, there are still reasons for shock. Most parents want not only children, but grandchildren as well. To learn that the sexual practice of one's child will not lead in that direction is disappointing. Perhaps more important, parents want their children to have lives that are as easy and happy as possible in an inevitably difficult world. Any realistic appraisal of this society indicates that homosexuals have enormous handicaps imposed on them. The hostility of parents is often one of these handicaps, but even when parents are supportive, the obstacles are still immense.

The church's teaching is one source of the social hostility that causes so much of the suffering of homosexuals. The question today is whether the church should continue the teaching that contributes so massively to this suffering or should recognize that homosexuals also have the right to love.

The church's unfortunate tendency to legalism has come to the fore on this topic more than on any other. Indeed, the quality of the discussion in recent years has been distressing. It seems that many people have simply assumed that homosexual practice is totally unacceptable and that therefore it must be forbidden in the Bible. When challenged, they have surveyed the entire literature to find every negative reference, actual or imagined. Whereas the Levitical code has generally been supposed to represent the kind of law set aside in the new covenant, its condemnation of homosexuals is often cited as evidence that homosexuality is not an acceptable practice among Christians. Most of those who use Leviticus against homosexuals do not take so seriously its much more central call for a year of Jubilee, in which property rights are to revert to the original owner. Paul's scattered and unsystematic comments are turned into a set of ethical rules and principles on this issue in a way that they are not on other topics.

It is particularly ironic that many Christians are prepared to set aside the direct and explicit teaching by Jesus on divorce but cling rigidly to obscure and questionable sources as justification for condemning homosexuality. There is nothing "biblical" or responsibly theological about such practice. The question to be asked is why so many Christians are searching so hard for biblical condemnation of homosexuality as opposed to the question of whether some biblical authors objected to it. That is why the study of homophobia is so important and appropriate today.

If the irrational fear and hostility that homosexuality arouses were overcome, the problem of acceptance would still not be easily solved. The question remains, What ideals should the church hold up before those who find themselves sexually attracted primarily to members of their own sex?

This chapter began with the ideal of a man and a woman who have only one sexual partner in their lives and whose sexual intercourse is exclusively within marriage. As mutual fulfillment of the partners was more fully recognized as essential to the ideal marriage, divorce and remarriage came to be accepted. The next step is for Christians to recognize that, as long as society encourages the delay of marriage far beyond the time of sexual maturation, it needs to approve temporary and provisional bondings that involve real mutual commitment and love.

The ideal of marriage, whether permanent or serial, has been deeply associated with the raising of children. For many homosexuals this is not a practical option. Some features of the classic Christian ideal are closed to them, so that even in a wholly unprejudiced society they will be in some measure deprived. On the other hand, many heterosexuals choose not to have children of their own or find that they are unable to do so. And, in an unprejudiced society, homosexuals are able to adopt children or even to bring up their own children. There are limitations built into the situation of the homosexual with respect to what has traditionally been sought in marriage; in a supportive society, however, these need not be extensive.

But even if some of the most meaningful possibilities of

life for the heterosexual are denied the homosexual, this certainly need not mean that additional burdens and restrictions should be imposed! It seems, rather, that the church's task is to help the homosexual envision positive scenarios for a happy future, scenarios that order the sexual life to wider purposes without simply denying or repressing it.

In a wholly unprejudiced society it would be pointless to mention any disadvantage of homosexuality if the division between heterosexuals and homosexuals were an absolutely clear and fixed one. But it is not. There are many people who have sexual attraction toward some members of both sexes. Today, sexual fulfillment has become for many people an end, even *the* end, in itself, encouraging bisexuals to act out both aspects of their feelings. But if sexuality is viewed in a wider context, then other matters besides desire should be considered in deciding on how to express one's sexuality. The potential joy of being a parent and of bringing up the child together with the other parent should be factored in. Further, in this highly prejudiced society, there are obviously other reasons for expressing only one's heterosexual feelings!

Factoring these considerations into the decision, however, should not involve social pressure toward marriage without regard to real feelings. The mere capability of having intercourse with a member of the opposite sex does not suffice to favor a heterosexual lifestyle over a homosexual one. If sexual desire for members of the same sex is clearly stronger, a heterosexual marriage will fall far short of the ideal. Often homosexually inclined spouses will be unfaithful, and even if they are faithful in act, important elements will be lacking in the marriage. The ideal includes a depth and warmth of personal relations that extend far beyond sexual intercourse but that are also hardly separable from sexual passion. Mere "performance" is not enough. The fulfillment of both partners will be truncated.

It is important to realize that this consideration is a relatively recent one. Through most of history, in most societies, procreation and property played the central roles in marriage, not mutual fulfillment. Death rates, especially among children, were high, and the replenishment or expansion of the population taking into account this high death rate took priority for the community as a whole over personal feelings. Raising a family was not an optional pleasure or privilege, but one's central duty to society. Although women other than prostitutes were strictly forbidden sexual activity outside of marriage, many societies had little objection to men seeking sexual pleasure with women other than their wives, or even with men, as long as they fulfilled their social duties of raising a family. Marriage itself was not, for most women or men, one option among others. Same-sex preferences were not seen as a reason for abstaining from marriage.

The global situation has now changed. Most countries, and the world as a whole, have more reason to be concerned about too many births than about too few. This is chiefly because modern medicine keeps alive many of the babies who in past ages would have died. This is a great gain in itself, but when it is not accompanied by other changes in cultural habits, the result is a terrible curse. Population growth rates point toward catastrophe!

In this context, the disinclination of a portion of the population to propagate the species is no longer something socially negative. Indeed, it relieves pressures, allowing those who do want to give birth to children more space in which to do so. Society as a whole, therefore, has no reason to push unwilling homosexuals to act as if they were heterosexual on this ground.

To sum up, there are two reasons for not continuing to pressure homosexually inclined men and women into heterosexual marriage, as society still does. First, the marriages are unlikely to meet the needs of either partner. Second, the traditional social reasons for urging marriage on the disinclined no longer apply.

If this reasoning is correct, it is time the church ceased to function as a religious support of social pressure toward undesirable heterosexual marriages. Instead, it should become the place to which troubled youth can turn for understanding and counsel. That cannot happen as long as legalism and homophobia prevail.

For those whose homosexual orientation is too strong to be denied, what is the best way to order their lives? For a few, perhaps, total celibacy is best. But surely for most, in a society that recognizes so clearly the positive value of sexual experience, this is not best. Their "burning" is unlikely to be redemptive either for themselves or for others. Also, the fragmentation of community leaves those who live alone peculiarly isolated and lonely. Even the church fails to include them readily and naturally. On the other hand, the too-often-selected alternative of promiscuity and casual sex also has marked disadvantages. The best choice for most is bonding, taking mutual responsibility for each other.

For homosexuals, as for heterosexuals, one ideal is that all sexual activity be with one partner in the context of lifelong commitment. But it is no more certain that the first such partnership can endure throughout life than in the case of heterosexual pairing. Nevertheless, to look toward lifelong mutual commitment as the goal is not misguided. Even in a society in which pressures are exerted more against such mutual commitments of homosexual couples than for them, many have succeeded. Today the agony of many a gay man dying of AIDS is eased by the faithful ministration of a partner who stays with him and ministers to him until death does them part. If the church threw the full weight of its moral support behind this ideal, more of these partnerships would succeed.

Perhaps most homosexual bondings will be more like the premarital bondings of heterosexuals than like marriages. But this is not necessarily the case. Homosexuals, like heterosexuals, do bond for life, and the church's role should be to encourage this.

Does this mean that homosexual couples ready to make

this lifelong commitment should be married? The answer depends on which of the elements in marriage is emphasized.

If marriage is seen as primarily the context for raising children, then most of these homosexual bondings would not be marriages, although even by this criterion some would be. But if other aspects of marriage are emphasized—permanence, social support, the bonding of families—then in principle marriage is open to homosexual couples as much as to heterosexual ones. Whether the word "marriage" is the best to use for permanent homosexual pairing is, in any case, not the crucial question. Temporary and permanent bondings should be distinguished, and the latter should be especially celebrated by the church, whatever name is chosen. It should have the same legal, moral, and religious status as heterosexual marriage.

The Current Debate

This approach to homosexuality is still seen by many Christians as failing to deal with Paul's picture of certain homosexual practices as degrading. But there is no inconsistency. Paul is surely correct that there are degrading homosexual practices. For example, the type he seems to have in mind in the famous Romans passage appears to be the ultimate in self-indulgence. But there are also degrading heterosexual practices. The issue should not be heterosexual versus homosexual, but humanizing versus degrading. How can this distinction be effectively made? This is an important question for Christians.

The sexual revolution has led to the widespread view that the only sexual acts that are objectionable are those in which one partner participates unwillingly or is not old enough to make a responsible decision. A second level of restriction can be made around faithfulness to covenants. If two people agree to an exclusive relationship, then sexual acts that break the covenant can be condemned. But Paul's point involves something else. Is it possible, despite the basic affirmation of sexual enjoyment, still to distinguish on other grounds between humanizing and degrading expressions?

Yes, such a distinction is possible and important, and can be formulated in such a way as to make sense of Paul's outburst. The needed distinction has to do with how sexuality is related to the rest of life. One trend in the sexual revolution celebrates the separation of sexuality from its immersion in the whole pattern of human relationships. Some think that the most complete sexual abandon is attained when the partners are merely physical objects for one another. There is an element in the male psyche that idealizes this completely impersonal sex, often associated with aggression and even sadism. It involves revolt against all social and societal restraints.

The pursuit of new pleasurable sensations involving the depersonalization of the partner can be imposed on an unwilling partner or on one who is made willing only by payment of money. Many proponents of the sexual revolution oppose this. But what if one partner, most often the woman, agrees to cooperate in sexual experimentation that is dehumanizing to her for fear that otherwise her husband will seek another woman or simply out of the desire to do her duty as wife? Does this kind of willingness render such sex acceptable? Emphatically not. Once sexual experience is sought for its own sake, rather than as a means of mutual enjoyment and of deepening personal relations, it can easily become degrading rather than humanizing.

But how is this related to Paul's reference to homosexual practices as illustrating sexual degradation? Once the quest for sexual experiences becomes an end in itself, rejecting all social and personal considerations, even primarily heterosexual men can extend their experimentation in ways that deny not only their social roles but even their dominant natural inclinations. They may want to add to their experience even what it is like to be a woman. As the extreme limit of turning the restricted good of sexual enjoyment into the absolute good to which all else is subordinated, these homosexual acts illustrate the gross idolatry against which Paul inveighs. This has nothing to do with sexual expressions of mutual affection between two women or two men who are personally committed to each other.

The goodness of sexuality does not mean that the pursuit of sexual sensations without regard for human relations and larger purposes is good. On the contrary. The righteous life is one in which sexual enjoyment is subordinated to other ends. We do not live in order to savor delicate tastes, to have emotional highs, or to enjoy sexual or religious ecstasies. These may come to us in the course of working with others toward the upbuilding of human community in anticipation of God's reign. If so, we have cause for gratitude. If we seek God's reign first, much else may be added to us. But this does not justify seeking first these other goods.

To affirm committed homosexual relationships is not, therefore, to condone what Paul depicted as the final outcome of idolatry. Instead, it is calling for a high level of personal discipline and commitment. What is wrong with the church's present stance is that by making no distinction between utterly self-indulgent and irresponsible pleasure-seeking and lifelong commitments, often made in the face of social contempt, it contributes to immorality among homosexuals. If every homosexual act is equally condemned, why adopt the more demanding lifestyle?

Furthermore, much of the least responsible behavior of homosexuals is engendered by low self-esteem. For this too the church shares major responsibility. To care for homosexuals, as the church professes to do, is to love and affirm them as homosexual persons, not despite their homosexuality. It is to ask of them just as much self-denial and self-discipline as it asks of heterosexuals, while offering as much sexual fulfillment and human happiness as they are capable of attaining in a context that is oriented primarily to the service of God through the service of human beings.

Some Christians who would agree with much of the above

are still convinced that homosexuality is not morally accept-able, that it is against God's intentions for human beings, that it violates something fundamental in the nature of things. These Christians may want to support individual homosexuals in any way they can and to avoid self-righteous and moralistic condemnation. But they are not prepared to support any affirmation by the church that there is a legiti-mate homosexual lifestyle. In their view, the only options for those who are homosexually inclined are transformation to heterosexuality or complete self-denial.

This deep-seated sense that homosexual activity violates something basic in the nature of things must be considered openly and fairly. It can be supported from the importance of heterosexuality in the evolutionary process; homosexual-ity has played no analogous role. In theological terms it appeals to the story of the Creation. God created man and woman. God created them for one another. That is what sexuality is all about. The mating of male and female fulfills the intent of creation. There is no analogous place for the mating of male with male or female with female. Even though there are no clear condemnations of all homosexual behavior in the Bible, all discussions of sexuality assume that the mating of male and female is normative.

It would probably be more accurate to say that the bibli-cal accounts are reflections of the same deep-seated sensibil-ity in their authors that is felt by such readers than that the accounts are the reason for this attitude among Christians. Nevertheless, the point is well taken. Although it is seri-ously misleading to say that the Bible condemns homosexu-ality, it is accurate to say that it looks on heterosexuality as normal and normative.

The question before Christians today is: What conclu-sions should we draw about present teaching from this his-torical fact? Does the way the Bible describes the creation of male and female tell us something about God's intentions for the church's dealings with homosexuals now? If so, what?

The mode of thinking that draws the conclusion that the church cannot condone any form of homosexual activity is similar to that of Roman Catholic natural-law thinking treated in chapter 2. One discerns in the dominant patterns a purpose which is then understood absolutistically as applying to all. One judges that because men and women are made for each other, analogous relations between men or between women are precluded.

It is important to see that a slightly different conclusion could be drawn. One could decide that because men and women are made for each other, celibacy is precluded. Jews have tended to draw this conclusion, but most Christians have not. The fact that both Jesus and Paul seem to have been celibate has encouraged Christians to think of celibacy as a noble estate to which some Christians are called.

Since an exception is made here to the general pattern derived from the story of the Creation, the question is whether other such exceptions cannot be made, specifically in favor of homosexual bondings. The refusal to do this seems to reflect the assumption that these bondings fall below the established norm. It is difficult not to conclude that the difference in judgment expresses deep-seated feelings that in fact have little to do with biblical authority.

There are other difficulties with drawing too many conclusions about sexual relations from the story of the Creation. Although the story in the first chapter of Genesis is almost gender neutral, the story in the second chapter is patriarchal to the core. The subordination of the wife to the husband is a far clearer implication of the Creation story than any rejection of homosexuality. Further, this subordination of the wife is even more pervasive of biblical texts than is the norm of heterosexuality.

If, today, Christians are prepared to repent of millennia-long patriarchal sexism, deeply rooted in Scripture, why should they cling to millennia-long patriarchal homophobia, much less explicitly supported in the Bible? Surely the answer must be found in personal feelings rather than in the Bible!

The issue about homosexuality that has recently confronted the church most insistently is whether homosexuals should be ordained as ministers. For the debate about homosexuality to have begun with this issue is unfortunate. Given the state of church teaching and practice on homosexuality in general, there are strong arguments against ordaining homosexuals to serve as parish ministers in most parishes. The only behavior the church declares to be acceptable on the part of the homosexual minister is total abstinence from sexual activity. Yet the church declares sexual enjoyment to be a gift of God. How can the minister embody and express both the goodness of sexuality and also the total abstinence that is demanded? Of course, the church also rightly teaches that one should order one's sexuality to higher purposes; so the minister can model this heroic self-sacrifice, precarious as that is. But if she or he refuses such abstinence, the church has no category for her or his behavior except "sin."

The church needs to establish an approved way of life for the sexually active homosexual. Once that is established, then homosexual ministers can be measured by that lifestyle just as heterosexual ministers are properly measured by their conformity to approved lifestyles. There may still be congregations that, for various reasons, some of them justified, express their preference for heterosexual pastors, but ordination should, in principle, be no problem.

The argument that the establishment of an approved lifestyle should come first is not intended to support prohibition of such ordination in the meantime. Even before correcting the official teaching, churches can make reasonable judgments about individuals who are dealing responsibly with their sexuality and about congregations that are ready to accept them. Homosexual ministers even have some advantage in ministry and evangelism in the homosexual community, a community badly in need of the church's ministry. In church bodies in which ordination is separated from appointment to a parish, the present obstacles to ordination are greatly reduced. The presence of some ordained homosexuals within the church should speed and facilitate the church's deliberation on the issue of homosexuality generally. But the awkwardness and inconsistency involved in the whole situation should be recognized, and this recognition should heighten the urgency of shifting from legalistic condemnation to expressing love through helping homosexuals realize the optimum possibilities that the situation allows.

Theological Reflections

The emphasis in this chapter has been on ordering sexuality to larger and more inclusive purposes. This is the key point, essential to a Christian approach to sexuality, that is lacking in the sexual revolution. It means that personal sacrifices are often called for, that realizing one's full sexual potential is not the primary goal. It means that married persons who discover that they are also sexually attracted to members of their sex are not always justified in exploring this aspect of their being. It means that just saying "no" is often the correct response to invitations and opportunities for additional sexual experience. It means that long periods of abstinence from sexual intercourse are sometimes required.

The most commonly accepted reason for self-denial is fidelity to a partner. That certainly is *a* major reason. But it often functions in connection with others. Christians are sometimes called to throw themselves into the work of the church or the struggle for peace and justice in ways that disrupt normal wedded life. The ideal is that the mutual commitment of the partners be such that they are ready to accept even long separations for purposes in which they both believe, with the confidence that each will remain faithful to the other. This is possible only if both believe that there are other things in life more important than sexual fulfillment and even than personal happiness in general.

This is all highly idealistic. Indeed, this whole chapter is about appropriate ideals for ordering human sexuality. Everyone knows that in fact intensive commitment by one spouse to what seems an overwhelmingly important cause can lead the other spouse to break the marriage. Too many have entered marriage with the expectation that their partner's first commitment should be to them. The church has allowed itself to abet this idolatry. Of course, the threat to the marriage should be an important consideration before deciding to dedicate oneself to a task, for a broken marriage is a serious loss, over and above the loss of sexual fulfillment. But for Christians, even the preservation of marriages cannot be the final determinant in a decision. The ideal marriage is one that supports its members to give themselves fully to the work to which they are called by God. Paul was not wrong in his concern about marriage to unbelievers. This aspect of marriage needs to be much more emphasized by the church than has been common in our psychology- and sex-centered age.

This idealistic approach is profoundly misunderstood if it is translated in a legalistic or moralistic way. The ideal is of sexual activity only within committed relations, serving the deepening and personalizing of these relations, and subordinating even these relations to larger purposes. This ideal is meaningful and could become more meaningful in the church if it were thoughtfully presented and joyfully embodied. But it does not imply that every deviation from the ideal is the violation of a moral law against which rules and sanctions should be enforced. Circumstances vary, and even the most faithful Christians will have to adapt the ideal to these circumstances. In addition, all fall short of the glory of God, and in this sense, in our sexual lives as well, we are all sinners. The adoption of this type of ideal will not end that.

But the adoption of the ideal would have practical effects. It would enable the church to offer serious moral guidance in this central aspect of life rather than leaving the field polarized between traditional legalists on the one side and advocates of the sexual revolution on the other. And it would express itself in open affirmation and sanctioning of both heterosexual and homosexual bondings other than heterosexual marriage. The time has come at least for open discussion of these changes. May the church find its voice!

A Challenge to Christian Opinion

The four chapters in this book have expressed definite and controversial opinions on some "matters of life and death." I hold many of these opinions with deep conviction, and I think that much is at stake. It would be very satisfying to me if church leaders agreed with me and threw their weight behind the proposals I advocate.

Nevertheless, while I feel that the conclusions to which I have come are correct, I am even more deeply convinced that within the church these issues should be openly and freely discussed. It seems evident that such matters of life and death are appropriate topics of Christian reflection. Yet the church has often avoided considering them except when compelled to treat them by practical issues concerning its own life and practice. The church, which should be in the lead in shaping public opinion, lags behind.

There are exceptions. There is a church voice that repeats traditional views, making them sometimes more rigid than they have been in the past. This church voice does play some role in relation to public opinion. But on the whole it is unreflective. Instead of seeing that we are in a new situation which requires rigorous and open-minded fresh thinking, it seems to seek justification, by a very selective use of the evidence, for positions taken long ago. We cannot expect this to be convincing to others or even to our own members. Indeed, they should not be convinced.

In this book I have tried to be as open and clear as possible about the kind of thinking that leads me to my conclusions. From my point of view this is responsible Christian thinking. It is *not* the only mode of responsible Christian thinking. It invites correction and even rebuttal. If this response can be one that takes seriously my approach, as well as its intention to be Christian, if it makes clear its own assumptions and its evidence and its justification for calling itself Christian, then the thinking of the church can be clarified and moved forward by the exchange. It is that advance, rather than the present polarization, that we so badly need.